MARKETING HOPE

Marketing Hope

Get-Rich-Quick Schemes in Siberia

Leonie Schiffauer

berghahn
NEW YORK • OXFORD
www.berghahnbooks.com

First published in 2019 by
Berghahn Books
www.berghahnbooks.com

Library of Congress Cataloging-in-Publication Data

Names: Schiffauer, Leonie, author.
Title: Marketing hope : get-rich-quick schemes in Siberia / Leonie Schiffauer.
Description: New York : Berghahn Books, 2019. | Includes bibliographical references and index.
Identifiers: LCCN 2019004495 (print) | LCCN 2019006790 (ebook) | ISBN 9781789200133 (ebook) | ISBN 9781789200126 (hardback : alk. paper)
Subjects: LCSH: Fraud--Russia (Federation)--Siberia. | Multilevel marketing--Russia (Federation)--Siberia. | Investments--Russia (Federation)--Siberia. | Capitalism--Russia (Federation)--Siberia.
Classification: LCC HV6699.R92 (ebook) | LCC HV6699.R92 S5273 2019 (print) | DDC 364.16/30957--dc23
LC record available at https://lccn.loc.gov/2019004495

British Library Cataloguing in Publication Data

A catalogue record for this book is available from the British Library

ISBN 978-1-78920-012-6 hardback
ISBN 978-1-78920-013-3 ebook

To my parents

Contents

Acknowledgements

It would have been impossible for me to write this book without the various forms of support and encouragement that I received from people who accompanied me over the past couple of years.

In particular I am grateful to Caroline Humphrey, who supervised my research for this book. I thank her for her close reading of my work, for all the advice she gave me, for the illuminating discussions we had and for her kindness, patience and reliability.

My research in Siberia was enabled through the support of my Buryat friends and informants. I thank them for their hospitality and generosity, for sharing their stories and ideas, for trusting me and for supporting me emotionally during my fieldwork. In particular, the Tsydenov family, Dolgorma Tsydenova, Erzhena Tsyremzhitova, Baiaskhalan Zhabe, Soelma Syrempilova, Nadezhda Tsybikova and Iuliia Grigor'eva have made my stay in Russia a warm, rich and unforgettable experience.

I want to thank all those who have discussed my ideas with me, asked important questions and enriched my thinking during the process of writing this book. Special thanks to Matteo Benussi, Elizabeth Turk and Nurul Huda Mohd Razif for this.

I am indebted to my parents Werner Schiffauer and Gertrud Hüwelmeier for teaching me to think critically and to take up challenges, for encouraging me to write this book and for many important pieces of advice regarding my research and writing.

Finally, I want to thank the Studienstiftung des deutschen Volkes and the Cambridge Commonwealth, European and International Trust for their financial support.

Note on Transliteration

For the transliteration of Russian terms, I use the American Library Association and the Library of Congress (ALA-LC) standard. I make exceptions only in cases when I cite from sources that use a different transliteration or in cases when the common transliteration of names or places differs, i.e. Buryats instead of Buriats.

Introduction

'Please come, I want to introduce you to an interesting person', my acquaintance Elena told me when she called me in the summer of 2011 during my first stay in Aga. I asked her who she wanted me to meet and the answer was that she would explain the details later, but I should make sure not to miss this great opportunity. We met on Aginskoe's main square, from where she brought me into a small office in the backroom of a shop. Here, Lobsan, a well-dressed man in his early thirties, was expecting me. He welcomed me enthusiastically and told me that, like Elena, he was working for Amway, a great international company. The office had a few chairs, a desk, a large television screen on one wall and a shelf with the basic Amway products – detergents, cleaning materials and nutritional supplements – on the other wall. I was asked to take a seat and Lobsan began to explain what Amway was all about: first and foremost, making a lot of money. In what it soon became clear was an attempt to recruit me, he drew the company's marketing plan in order to illustrate step by step how I could quickly increase my sales volume, attract further salespeople and earn bonus payments. Then Lobsan switched on the screen to show me a short video of an American distributor who had become rich thanks to Amway. The man in the video took the spectator on a tour around his luxurious home, to his swimming pool surrounded by palms and to his car park, while praising the company for the opportunities it had given to him. Switching off the video, Lobsan turned to me again and said that this must have certainly convinced me that Amway was a business that offered great prospects. As a start, I should sign up (at a cost of 1,500 roubles (around $23)) and, most importantly, begin to actively consume and familiarize myself with the Amway products. Elena nodded in affirmation. She had only recently started her Amway business, she said, but with the help of Lobsan, who was her 'sponsor', the person who had recruited her into the scheme, she had quickly understood the benefits the company offers. With shining eyes, Elena asked me whether I would sign the contract immediately and Lobsan jumped to her aid, saying that it would be great to work with me. A few minutes later, feeling slightly guilty for having disappointed them by turning down their offer, I stepped out into the square's sunlight, puzzled by what I had seen. The promise of great wealth seemed to stand in stark contrast to the small wooden houses surrounding me and to the cows grazing on the side of the road. The American villa in the video appeared so very distant to me in the light of my whole experience of Aga, a small district in southeastern Siberia, where money is as scarce as experience of the world beyond the region. Apparently, however, Lobsan and Elena had fully embraced the dream and believed that the company offered them a glorious future.

Multilevel marketing (MLM) and pyramid schemes are flourishing in Aga. Their promise is to make people rich. According to the companies that push the schemes, the way to wealth and happiness is easy: all one needs to do is to register and to recruit further people into the schemes. Representatives of at least fifteen companies try to persuade their friends and relatives to join their schemes. They claim to offer an economic alternative in one of Russia's remote rural regions and encourage people to dream of a better future. For the vast majority, however, the dream of a life in luxury will never come true.

MLM and pyramid schemes are economic forms that structurally resemble each other closely, but whereas MLM is legal in most parts of the world, pyramid schemes are generally considered to be a financial scam. MLM is a huge business with around 90 million individuals worldwide representing direct selling companies such as Amway, Avon, Mary Kay Cosmetics, Herbalife or Tupperware and a sales volume of nearly US$189,641 million in 2017 (World Federation of Direct Selling Associations 2018a). The companies built on this model have no retail outlets for their products, most of which are beauty and health-related, but sell them via independent salespeople directly to the customer. The salespeople, often called 'distributors', do not receive a salary, but a commission on their sales. Moreover, they can earn money by recruiting subcontractors into their scheme because they also receive a commission on the sales of their downlines. Thus, distributors engage in both selling and persuading others to participate in the schemes. Only if they are successful in these endeavours they will be rewarded financially for their efforts.

The idea of MLM originated in the United States, where it gained popularity after the Second World War. It is underpinned by a capitalist ideology that openly promotes the American Dream. Companies acclaim the possibility to rise from rags to riches by joining them. They claim to provide the opportunity to make a fortune to everyone, regardless of education, ethnicity or professional experience. Everyone is invited to join the schemes and to become a businessman or businesswoman, and success or failure are said to depend solely on individual effort. Today, this globalizing industry makes most of its sales outside the United States with huge markets in Asia, Europe and Latin America (World Federation of Direct Selling Associations 2018a).

Pyramid schemes are global phenomena as well, but, unlike MLM, they are considered to be a form of crime in most legislative systems. Pyramid scheme operators recruit unsuspecting investors with the promise of high returns. They claim to run successful business projects, but in fact early investors are paid with the money collected from later investors. Products and services may be presented in order to mask the pyramid structure, but sales play only a marginal role, if any at all, in the schemes' compensation formula. Essentially, pyramid schemes are money-transfer schemes that benefit a small number of people at the top of the pyramid, while resulting in an eventual loss of money for the majority of investors. The rules regarding recruitment and recoupment of money vary, but whether or not one makes money depends almost entirely on one's position in the pyramid. A pyramid scheme may survive for several years, but, sooner or later, when growth stagnates, it will collapse.

After the fall of the Iron Curtain, MLM swept the formerly socialist countries and Russia quickly became a huge market for direct sales (Stanley 1996; World Federation of Direct Selling Associations 2018a). Simultaneously with the spread of MLM, a wave of Ponzi[1] and pyramid schemes made headlines during the 1990s across the postsocialist world. Schemes in Albania, Romania and Russia attracted millions of investors with the promise of high returns on their investments. Returns, however, were paid with the money of subsequent investors, so that eventually, when investments dried up, all the pyramids collapsed. Pyramid schemes keep popping up in Russia, many of them masked as lucrative business projects under the guise of MLM. According to the Russian Ministry of the Interior, more than 160 pyramid schemes were operating in the country in 2014, which resulted in a loss of US$46 million for their victims (Zamakhina 2015). Until 2016, there was no clear legislation with regard to pyramid schemes in Russia. Only after their collapse, when the scam had become obvious, could initiators of pyramid schemes be legally persecuted (Eremina and Biianova 2015). In 2016, in an attempt to fight the problem of pyramid schemes more effectively, a new law was released that declared them illegal.

As in other parts of the world, it is difficult for people to distinguish pyramid scams from MLM because their multilayered pyramid structure, the promises of the schemes' charismatic leaders, their methods of recruitment and the logics with which they operate appear very similar. In many cases the boundaries between MLM and pyramid schemes are blurred and MLM companies are frequently accused of being pyramid schemes. MLM may be seen as less harmful than pyramid schemes because less money is at stake. But although MLM is legal in Russia and many other countries, it is a highly contested industry everywhere that it appears.

This study is concerned with the local manifestation of a global industry and with the local manifestation of a type of fraud modelled upon this industry. I am interested to see how MLM and pyramid schemes translate into a postsocialist environment and how they affect this environment. The study explores how companies manage to recruit enormous numbers of ordinary people as their representatives, as advocates of their interests and missionaries of the American Dream, despite the fact that these highly contested economic forms make exaggerated promises, put strains on social relationships and make a few people rich at the expense of the vast majority of participants. By taking a close look at MLM and pyramid schemes, I suggest, we can better understand how capitalist ideology gains support at the periphery and how capitalist values penetrate social structures.

MLM and pyramid schemes can be seen as radical forms of market ideology and are therefore particularly well suited to reveal several of capitalism's key features and ideas. The schemes are radical in the sense that their representatives promote capitalist values aggressively and communicate them bluntly. An investigation of this radical form of capitalism in a postsocialist environment, I suggest, is particularly illuminating. It is through MLM and pyramid schemes that ordinary people in the Siberian countryside begin seeing capitalism not only as a necessary way of coping with harsh realities, but also as an economic system of possibilities. Companies encourage people to imagine alternative futures and, most importantly, they claim to enable them to act in the here and now towards achieving their material dreams. The vast majority of participants in MLM and pyramid schemes have never previously imagined that they might come into riches. The schemes introduce speculative thinking and capitalist values to a place where people grew up with socialist ideology and values contrary to those proclaimed by MLM and pyramid schemes. Therefore, by studying MLM and pyramid schemes in postsocialist rural Russia, we can see most clearly the fascination that capitalism exerts over people, how capitalist thinking pervades and shapes social logics, and how speculative behaviour proliferates.

Aga

Aga is located east of Lake Baikal, between the Onon and Ingoda Rivers, near the borders with China and Mongolia. The district is one of the two Buryat regions outside Buryatia, which, prior to its incorporation into Zabaykalsky Krai in 2008, had autonomous status.[2] As I will show below, Aga's autonomous status played an important role for the district's economic development after socialism. With a population of 77,000 spread across 20,000 square kilometres, Aga is a sparsely populated rural region. Most of my research I conducted in its district centre, the town Aginskoe, which lies 150 kilometres southwest of the region's capital, Chita. I chose Aga as my field site because of the density of MLM and pyramid schemes in this remote and rural part of Russia.

In the following, I will introduce my field site. Knowledge of the particular social structures and economic development of the region are essential to an understanding of how MLM and pyramid schemes have proliferated so successfully in this part of the world. The brief outline presented here will be elaborated in Chapter 1 in relation to the economic situation and in Chapter 4 in relation to sociocultural dynamics.

Aga's population consists of 62.6 per cent Buryats, 35.1 per cent Russians and small minorities of Tatars, Ukrainians, Armenians and Bashkirs.[3] In the town Aginskoe, with its population of around 17,000 inhabitants, Buryats number around 70 per cent, which is slightly higher than in the district as a whole.[4] The Buryats, a Mongolian people, have lived as nomadic pastoralists in the regions around Lake Baikal for many centuries. The population formerly consisted of various tribes and only after the Russian conquest of the territory did they begin to perceive of themselves as an ethnic group. In the 1640s, the first Russians came to the territories east of Lake Baikal and during the 1650s and 1660s, they took control over the area (Nimaev 2004: 43). According to the chronicler Toboev, large groups of Khori Buryats moved eastwards to the territories of today's Aga in the early nineteenth century. The reason for this migration was that Russian settlers were given the land along the Ingoda, Ulunga and Ture Rivers that these Buryats had formerly inhabited. They moved to the Aga and Onon valleys and, in 1837, the Aga Buryats split formally from the Khori *vedomstvo* (administrative unit) that was part of Verkhneudinsk district (today's Burytia). Through formal integration into the Nerchinsk district (today's Zabaykalsky Krai), a territorial and political unit separate from the larger mass of Buryats was established, which was then governed through its own 'Steppe Duma' (Toboev 2011: 11–28).

Aga's centre, the town Aginskoe, was founded at the turn of the nineteenth century. It developed around a post station, administrational yurts and the first wooden buildings being erected by the Tataurovs, the first Russian settlers in the region who had come to Siberia in search of land and freedom (Gongorov 2002; Tataurov 2006). The Tataurovs were peasants and engaged in trade relationships with local Buryats. They learned the Buryat language and also intermarried with the Buryats (Tataurov 2006). In 1811, the Agin Buddhist monastery was founded, which became an important religious centre. In 1859, an Orthodox church was built. The town Aginskoe was located on the road to China and Mongolia and therefore became an important trading point. Every year, Chinese and Mongolian traders as well as traders from various places in the area came to the market in Aginskoe, which was the largest in the region (Tumunov 2006: 11). Very few Buryats at that time lived in stable settlements and most moved around the steppes living in felt yurts (Linkhovoin 2012: 199).

When the Soviets came to power, the Buryats were forced to give up their nomadic way of life and both Russians and Buryats had to reorganize agriculture and pastoralism according to central plans of collectivization. By the mid 1930s, the majority of households had been incorporated into units that served as the basis for collective farms (Shagdarov and Dorzhiev 1971: 18). A considerable number of Buryats fled from Aga to Mongolia and China after the revolution in order to escape economic difficulties or enforced collectivization.[5] Those who owned larger numbers of cattle or who belonged to the clergy were persecuted, killed or banned from their homelands (Tumunov 1993: 43–74). Throughout the following decades, Aga developed according to socialist planning and ideology. Agriculture and herding remained the base of the local economy, but the socialist government established a mining industry in the region along with a number of further industrial enterprises and transport and communication services (Shagdarov and Dorzhiev 1971: 8–28). The Communist Party sent political workers, teachers and cultural activists to Aga in order to create local cadres and to explain Lenin's ideas and the Party's aims to the people. Additional schools were established in the countryside and later on, libraries, cinemas and cultural venues were built.

The demise of the Soviet Union was followed by a severe economic crisis across the whole of its territory. The situation in Aga was particularly precarious. Its GDP reached merely 31 per cent of the Russian average in 2003 as it depended mainly on agricultural production, for which important markets were lost after the collapse of the Soviet system (Nezavisimyi Institut Sotsial'noi Politiki 2004). The majority of collective farms could no longer survive without state subsidies and dissolved. As a result, it became increasingly difficult to make a living in the countryside. In the search for alternatives, many people left rural regions in order to find employment in towns or cities. Like other towns and cities across Russia, Aginskoe grew significantly during this period due to the influx of people from the villages. People had to cope not only with the demise of a whole ideology around them, but also with economic insecurity and the struggle to make a living.

It was towards the end of the 1990s that the economic situation in the district improved significantly thanks to a deal between the local politician Zhamsuev and his important personal connections in Moscow. Aga's autonomous status allowed the creation of a special economic zone and the district became a tax haven within Russia. This legal arrangement brought large revenues to the district for a few years and made a paradisiac island within Zabaykalsky Krai. Roads were paved, public institutions like schools, the administration and kindergartens moved to smart new buildings, sports facilities were established, memorial sites were built and even a small branch of the Buryat State University was founded. There was so much money, as is vividly remembered today, that the local authorities had difficulty spending it all. The cash injection came to an end with the loss of autonomous status, but in comparison to the surrounding regions, Aga still evokes the impression of a prosperous place.

Coming to Aginskoe, the largest of the district's three towns, one passes the bronze statue of Balzhin Khatan, the legendary mother of the Khori Buryats, framed by an ethnic style arch situated in front of the modernist architecture of the small theatre. The road leading towards the town's centre is framed by small wooden houses of the kind that house most people in rural Siberia. Due to the recent influx of people, many houses are relatively new, which makes the town look rather tidy. Most of the houses are divided into two or three rooms with a wood-fired oven in the middle of the house. Some households have installed water pumps in their yards, while others have to fetch water from wells. A canalization system was built in the town during the good years, but few buildings are connected to it. On the way to the town's central square, it is not unusual that one sees cows crossing the road. Cows are left to themselves during the day to graze in the hilly steppes surrounding Aginskoe and find their way home in the evening. For many families in Aga, cattle, as well as vegetable plots, are an important part of the subsistence economy. The main road, with its dusty sidewalks, leads to the square with a fountain, banks and flower beds. Surrounded by little cafeterias and shops, hairdressers and banks, this is the centre of the town. The Orthodox church on the south side of the square, which had been converted to a cinema during Soviet times, was restored to its original function in the early 1990s. To the square's west, a spacious museum has been built where visitors can see a yurt and its interiors, traditional Buryat clothing that today is worn only on holidays, agricultural tools that the Russians have brought to the region, and photographs of the Steppe Duma and of the Soviet era collective farms. In front of the museum, an 'alley of fame' lines the road with busts of Buryat heroes who defended their nation during the Second World War. East of the square is a small market crammed with Chinese clothes and footwear. Over its entrance door, a loudspeaker blasts popular Russian music from the radio into the streets. Within a few hundred metres north and west of the square, the town's two event venues are located: the House of Culture and a concert hall. Buryat artists from Mongolia, China and Buryatia come to the town to give concerts or theatre and dance performances. Buryat holidays such as Sagaalgan (New Year) are celebrated here as well as holidays of national importance, for example, Victory Day (celebrating the Soviet victory over fascist Germany). From the small bus station in the centre of town, people can travel on minibuses over bumpy roads to the district's villages or, by taking the federal route, can reach Chita, which lies on the Trans-Siberian Railway and also has a small airport, within two hours.

In the town's public sphere, both Russian and Buryat are spoken. Everyone speaks Russian fluently, whereas people's knowledge of Buryat, a Mongolian language, mostly depends on how much Buryat is used in their families. Those with a profound knowledge of Buryat usually speak Buryat at home and with relatives, while they speak a Buryat-Russian mix in public spaces and with their friends. Buryat language is used for announcements during cultural events and there is also a newspaper issued in Buryat. There are no significant ethnic tensions in Aga and ethnicity is not a topic present in public discourse. Whenever I asked people about interethnic relationships, they found the question rather strange. They answered that it makes no difference to them whether someone is Buryat or Russian. Despite this stance, which certainly owes a lot to the socialist rhetoric of interethnic friendship, I observed that ethnic separation was maintained. The question of language often determines the choice of school to which parents send their children. Thus, schools in which the Buryat language is taught are predominantly attended by Buryat children. Cultural life, including theatre, concerts, dance performances and the celebration of public holidays, is clearly dominated by Buryat traditions and Russians hardly ever attend these events. The local job market is heavily structured by kinship relations that are of great social significance in Buryat society. Therefore, several institutions (e.g. the administration) are dominated by the Buryat population, whereas others (e.g. some of the schools and nurseries) are in the hands of Russians.

Today's Aginskoe is a showpiece for those who wish to project a positive image of the region. However, the impression of a prosperous little town is somewhat deceptive. With the administrative restructuring of 2008, the district lost its autonomy and also its special economic status. The flow of money dried up and today the facades of the smart new buildings are crumbling, the heating in public buildings is turned off too early, the better-quality computers and printers have been taken to Chita, and state employees sometimes receive their salaries several months late. There is little money and the crisis in the Russian economy, which stemmed from the fall of the price of oil in 2014 and from the EU sanctions imposed in 2014 as a result of the conflict in Ukraine, began to show its effects at the time of my research. Job opportunities are limited and salaries are extremely low. In addition, Zabaykalsky Krai is among Russian regions with the highest levels of household indebtedness. Debt has become an increasing concern for people since banks started granting consumer credit widely in the aftermath of the 2008 global financial crisis. Young and well-educated people, in particular, see no future in staying in the region. They are drawn to the cities, mainly to Chita, Ulan-Ude and Irkutsk. Some search for jobs in China or Mongolia; others dream of living in Moscow or even further west. There is considerable out-migration, while at the same time the town remains a magnet for people from the villages who move to Aginskoe in the hope of finding employment.[6]

The first MLM schemes began appearing in Aga in the late 1990s, but they became popular only after 2010, mainly through the activities of Amway representatives. The American company offers personal and domestic care items such as toothpaste, vitamins and all-purpose cleaners. However, it was less the products that attracted people to the company than the job opportunities it offered. Amway advertised these opportunities successfully through local training seminars paired with clear guidance for new distributors. The company promised to teach people entrepreneurial thinking that would enable them to make big money.

During the time of my research from 2014 to 2015, at least ten MLM companies were operating in the district, all of which market similar products. To give a precise number is difficult because the presence of the companies depends on the activity and also on the number of local salespeople, both of which may fluctuate heavily. Some companies were represented through a small number of salespeople, whereas others, such as Amway, had a considerable salesforce in Aga numbering at least several hundred distributors. Some of the salespeople set up small offices from which they organized their selling and advertising, whereas others tried to recruit people online or sell products in domestic spaces. I heard of companies that had salespeople in Aga prior to my arrival, but were no longer represented by anyone during the time of my research, and I also witnessed the appearance of new companies. The majority of MLM companies that I encountered in Aga operate transnationally. They have headquarters in the United States, Europe, China or Russia and have national and regional branches and a widely dispersed salesforce in several countries. They spread mainly on the initiative and through the recruitment activities of their salespeople. In Aga, the MLM schemes appear mostly through visitors from Irkutsk, Ulan-Ude or Chita who are originally from the district or have relatives in Aga and who recruit family members and other acquaintances.

Around the time when MLM became massively popular, several Ponzi and pyramid schemes also attracted large numbers of people in Aga. Local operators of these schemes promised people high returns on their investments. Those who were among the first to put money into the schemes were paid by the investments of those who followed. Two of the biggest schemes, MMM and LBM, collapsed in 2012 and 2013 respectively and left many people indebted to the banks from which they had borrowed the money that they had paid into the schemes. Details on the nature of these schemes will be given in Chapter 2. Here I simply want to point to the fact that something like a gambling craze had occurred in Aga before my arrival in 2014. The pyramid schemes that were operated in Aga during the time of my research attracted far fewer people and far less investment than did MMM and LBM. Their operators claimed to represent serious companies running profitable business projects and denounced the fraudulent schemes that had collapsed. They claimed, and at least some of them seriously believed, that they represented MLM companies that worked according to the same model as Amway. These pyramid schemes distributed products that very much resembled the products usually sold by MLM companies. However, the products were of little or no significance in their schemes, which depended on the investment of large sums of money. The pyramid schemes appeared in Aga in the same ways as MLM, through representatives of distant companies who had been recruited by relatives from the cities. Some schemes had been discovered by local people searching the internet for business opportunities. The local operators of the pyramid schemes, just like the salespeople of the MLM companies, attended seminars across Russia to get instructions or training and communicated with the founders and other participants of the schemes online. It is important to note that the first households in Aga were connected to the internet in around 2011. Thus, the pyramid boom coincided with access to the internet, which played an important role in the proliferation of pyramid schemes, much as it did for the organization of MLM.

Everyone in Aga knows about MLM (*setevoi biznes*) and pyramid schemes (*piramidy*), and has been involved in one way or another. People have either tried to sell products, they have made investments, purchased products, attended business seminars or at least have close relatives who participated and repeatedly invited them to do so as well. The peak of recruitment was clearly over in 2014, when I arrived in Aga and there was a great deal of disillusionment. Most people who had hoped to become rich through MLM or pyramid schemes had realized that this was very unlikely to happen. Despite this disillusionment, there was also widespread uncertainty regarding the potential of MLM and pyramid schemes to offer opportunities to people. After all, there were some people who claimed to have made money in such schemes and, in some cases, this was clearly true. Moreover, there were those who still fervently believed that the business they were pushing could bring great financial reward to themselves and others. Active MLM distributors believed that those unsuccessful in MLM had simply not worked hard enough and the operators of pyramid schemes attributed the collapse of previous pyramid schemes not to their pyramidal structure, but to the insincerity of their founders and operators. It was through the continuous efforts of these local distributors and operators, mainly elderly Buryat women, that both MLM and pyramid schemes kept attracting new recruits, although in far fewer numbers than in the years preceding my research.

Postsocialist Capitalism

The end of Soviet socialism left capitalism unchallenged as the contemporary way of organizing the economy. There is no longer an ideological alternative powerful enough to seriously question or challenge capitalism. Today, there are very few places that are not somehow affected by global flows of goods, services and money. Nevertheless, despite increasing economic globalization and interconnectedness, it is important to consider that capitalism has various histories and therefore various faces in different parts of the world. Anthropologists have shown that capitalism does not eradicate local economic systems and patterns of economic activity, but that it merges with them in multiple ways (Blim 2000; Watson 2006; Yang 2000).

Scholars of postsocialist economies have contributed significantly to our knowledge of the form of capitalism that emerged from the turbulent changes following the collapse of the Soviet Union. Capitalism arrived as shock therapy, implemented from above as a set of neoliberal reforms and with little regard to social and cultural realities. Anthropologists who studied the consequences of this restructuring of the economy according to the neoliberal model have shed light on how this period of profound transformation has shaped people's everyday lives and social relations.

The demise of the Soviet Union was followed by severe economic upheaval accompanying processes of decollectivization and privatization. In the countryside, many collective farms dissolved, triggering migrations to district centres such as Aginskoe, as well as to the cities. Many people could not work their privatized lands because they did not have the machinery or lived too far away from their property. Consequentially, much land was left unproductive, leading to a drop in agricultural output across formerly socialist countries (Hann 2003; Verdery 1996). In Russia, some of the collective farms resisted dissolution and continued to exist under an altered form of management. However, these farms faced serious economic difficulties without state subsidies and struggled to pay their staff monetary salaries (Humphrey 1998).

Decollectivization provided few benefits for ordinary rural people, forcing them to look for economic alternatives. Towns and cities grew significantly as people arrived from the countryside. However, the situation in urban centres was also difficult. State enterprises collapsed, major industries were closed down and the urban infrastructure saw major breakdowns. Unemployment soared in cities like Ulan-Ude and poverty increased along with rates of criminality (Humphrey 2007). The people who profited from this situation were largely those who had been in dominant positions during Soviet times and who had the personal social networks that were essential to getting things done in newly capitalist Russia (Ledeneva 1998, 2006).

The process of privatization in Russia led to increased inequality and left many people with feelings of injustice, deprivation and, perhaps above all, uncertainty (Burawoy and Verdery 1999). The Soviet ideology and along with it a whole economic system simply disappeared. State benefits that had been generous during Soviet times were cut and suddenly people were expected to pay for necessities such as heat and electricity. Money was needed urgently, but it was very difficult to earn. Moreover, inflation was rampant in the 1990s. In both the countryside and the cities, people relied heavily on their vegetable plots. Under these circumstances, a barter economy developed on the macroeconomic as well as the microeconomic level. Collective farms, corporations and people traded with each other and in many cases such trade was eased by systems of coupons or alternative currencies (Anderson 2000; Humphrey 2000; Woodruff 1999).

The void left by the collapse of the old system opened niches for new economic activities. Petty trade was one of the few ways in which rural people could earn money in the 1990s. During Soviet times, private trade had been heavily restricted as it was seen as an unproductive and speculative activity. In the difficult situation of the 1990s, people were pushed into trading in order to make a living. Immense numbers of new traders crossed international borders and brought goods from China or Central Asia to Russia. Their activities were heavily dependent upon contacts with border guards, and networks of cooperation were thus created at the borders. This trade was at first improvised and perceived as chaotic 'disorder' (Humphrey 1999). At the other end of the socioeconomic spectrum were the businesspeople known as the 'New Russians': cosmopolitan entrepreneurs – bankers, brokers and managers – who quickly became affluent during this turbulent period of transformation and were able to embrace a consumerist lifestyle that was way beyond what ordinary citizens could afford. These urban entrepreneurs embodied the ideals of a new neoliberal discourse that had begun to permeate Russia at that time (Yurchak 2003).

The economic situation has certainly improved since the 1990s, albeit unevenly across Russia. However, unlike most Western parts of the country, many regions in Siberia, including the Zabaykalsky Krai, continue to depend on subsidies from Moscow. In some parts of Russia, such as Aga, regional autonomy in combination with the informal networks of power that are so characteristic of Russia (Ledeneva 2013) have had a significant impact on economic development. New private banks have played an important part in the shaping of economic realities in postsocialist countries. With regard to Russia, these mechanisms have received little attention, but it has been shown that in Mongolia new credit schemes for pastoralists have resulted in an increasing burden of debt on households (Sneath 2012). The situation in

Siberia is similar and, as in Mongolia, loan sharks and pawn shops are omnipresent (cf. Højer 2012). New ways of accessing money through loans paired with new means of payment such as credit cards (cf. Guseva 2008) have contributed significantly to changing attitudes to consumption. Household indebtedness is a serious problem in several of Russia's provinces, and the illicit practices of private banks that sell debts to collector agencies and exert severe pressure on debtors persist.

The appeal of MLM and pyramid schemes needs to be understood within the context of postsocialist economic developments. MLM and pyramid schemes seemingly offer not only the opportunity to make money in an environment where most people are struggling with debts, but also do so in a way that seems to contrast with the exclusivity of much of the postsocialist economy: an opportunity is offered to people regardless of their position in social hierarchies; the job of selling and/or recruiting can be done everywhere, in the countryside as well as in the cities, and may be combined with other jobs or familial duties; and the companies offer not only a clear ideology that fits the neoliberal discourse and role models, but also guidance, including a recipe for success. In short, MLM and pyramid schemes seem to offer an opportunity as well as a way out of the difficulties people are struggling with. All of this appears extremely attractive – as long as the schemes' representatives manage to sustain the idea that what they offer will bring the imagined reward.

Popular Finance

Contemporary capitalism is increasingly defined by the ever-more rapid circulation of money. Over the past few decades, production-centred state-based capitalism has shifted to a capitalism that is characterized by transnational flows of money and that is less and less tied to territory. Today, economic environments everywhere are affected by complex financial transactions in high finance, such as the buying and selling of derivatives (LiPuma and Lee 2004). Anthropologists interested in tracing these changes have applied ethnographic methods to the study of the centres of finance such as Wall Street and the Chicago Board of Trade, and have conducted research among investment bankers and traders (Ho 2009a; Miyazaki 2013; Zaloom 2006). These studies, among others, have yielded valuable insights into how financial markets work and how they are made, have shown the motivations and logics according to which elite financial actors act, and have revealed the significance of capitalist temporality (see also Appadurai 2013). New approaches suggest taking into view a wider range of sites where speculation occurs and to consider also the financial practices of non-elite members of society (Bear, Birla and Puri 2015). The authors argue that speculative activity has become popular with the democratization of finance, and studying such activity in emerging markets can make an important contribution to the understanding of capitalism in its contemporary form. My study of MLM and pyramid schemes in Siberia picks up and develops the focus on speculative capitalism at the periphery. It shows how ordinary people are captured by the imagination of material wealth and how the anticipation of possible futures leads them to engage in highly contested economic activities. The data I present in this book provides an example of how markets are made from the bottom of the pyramid with a focus on the socioeconomic mechanisms that determine their growth.

A focus on popular finance is important because the development of financial markets and the activities of financial elites have consequences far away from the centres of finance where large-scale speculation takes place. Increasing speculation in financial markets and the opacity of new forms of wealth may be reflected in everyday social and economic practices, as Jean and John Comaroff (2001) have argued convincingly. The authors suggest that capitalism at the millennium is characterized by the fact that it marginalizes at the same time as it includes people, depending on whether they master its technologies. These capitalist realities give rise to what they call 'occult economies'. Money magic, pyramid schemes and prosperity gospels proliferate across the world, especially in societies that have recently seen significant social and economic change. Occult economies, the Comaroffs argue, could be seen as an attempt to make sense of the enigma of great wealth by those who cannot participate in the 'conventional' spheres of business or finance. Similarly, Detlev Krige (2012), who studied MLM and pyramid schemes in South Africa, argues that risk taking in pyramid schemes is hardly different from the risk taking that lies at the basis of commodities and futures trading in global financial markets. Krige also points to the important connection between the recent incorporation of large parts of the South African population into the banking system, the popularization of finance and the proliferation of MLM and pyramid schemes.

A good indication that the proliferation of pyramid schemes is linked to macroeconomic change is provided by the postsocialist case. Katherine Verdery (1996), for instance, understands the popularity of the Romanian Caritas scheme in the early 1990s as a response to the economic crisis that followed the end of socialism. She argues that skyrocketing inflation, a drastic drop in income and problematic access to loans drew people towards such schemes. Likewise, Smoki Musaraj (2011) sees the deregulation of financial markets in the course of postsocialist transformation as giving rise to the Albanian schemes of the 1990s. Furthermore, Musaraj regards inflows of cash, most notably immigrant remittances, as playing a crucial role for the proliferation of the schemes. She argues that the materiality of the money that circulated as stacks of cash was important because it made the magical mechanism of the schemes concrete and visible in the public domain. Neoliberal reforms in Mexico, Thailand and China have also been seen by scholars as a significant cause of the popularization of MLM business from the late 1980s onwards in these countries (Cahn 2011; Jeffery 2001; Wilson 2004).

The surge of MLM and pyramid schemes can be assumed to reflect macroeconomic tendencies rather than being disconnected from them. However, the schemes are not parallel universes of the poor or a local mirror of the 'real' economy; rather, they are part of the global flows of money that characterize neoliberal capitalism. MLM is a huge industry and the founders of some of these companies are millionaires and politically highly influential. Amway's founder families, for example, entertain close connections to the Republican Party. In 2017, Elisabeth DeVos, daughter-in-law of Amway founder Richard DeVos, was elected U.S. Secretary of Education under President Donald Trump, who himself has promoted MLM through the Trump Network (Jones 2011: 2). Similarly, pyramid scams are not necessarily started by petty criminals at the local level, but may be initiated by financiers with influential connections such as Bernard Madoff. Pyramid scheme participants in South Africa, for example, have been found to include doctors, lawyers and company managers, and such schemes operate from prestigious business addresses (Krige 2012: 73–74). In both the Romanian and Albanian cases, prominent politicians supported pyramid schemes (Verdery 1996; Musaraj 2011). MLM and pyramid schemes come into being locally through the activities of local people, but they constitute networks, sometimes reaching across borders and connecting people across large distances. Thus, we have to pay attention to the particular circumstances under which they emerge locally as much as to the global connections that make them a universal phenomenon.

MLM and pyramid schemes introduce economic forms to the Siberian countryside that link ordinary people to faraway places. The idea of being connected, and especially the idea of being connected to an economically powerful elsewhere, is crucial for the appeal of the schemes. The imagination of how these new ties could account for flows of money to rural Siberia and how being part of an international business community could bring about the desired rewards is key in MLM and pyramid schemes. MLM and pyramid schemes open new imaginative horizons that have both a spatial and a temporal dimension. My study deals with these imaginaries and explores how they shape economic activities. However, my analysis is not restricted to the small group of those who believe fervently in the schemes. Notably, their daily work consists of convincing others – those who do not yet dream, who dream only reluctantly or who have given up dreaming – to join their companies. Therefore, it is crucial to take into account the social space in which they work. How are people attracted to speculative practices? How is speculation embedded in its social and cultural environment? And what are the social logics that give rise to speculative behaviours? Virtually all studies of MLM focus only on those who are actively involved and therefore can only partially reveal the contested and highly problematic nature of the industry. Unlike experts at the centres of finance, those who push MLM and pyramid schemes daily confront others who are critical of their practice. It is these encounters in which imaginaries are constantly questioned and challenged and that make it necessary to reaffirm their belief again and again. Thus, this study seeks not only to give insights into the imaginary worlds of those who push the schemes most actively, but also to discuss the social realities in which dreams are learned, communicated, negotiated, questioned and shattered.

Gambling or Business?

When risky financial investment takes place outside the spheres of what is perceived as professional finance, it is commonly associated with gambling. In contrast to finance, gambling is understood as an unprofessional and somewhat disreputable leisure activity. What takes place in the sphere of business or finance, on the other hand, is accepted by most people as professional and legitimate. This distinction, of course, is constructed. De Goede (2005), for example, shows how during the nineteenth and twentieth centuries, the notion of finance was separated from that of gambling as part of the proliferation of the capitalist market logic. As the 2008 global financial crisis has clearly shown, financial markets are not under full control and financial professionals may behave like gamblers. Anthropological studies have also contributed to challenging the myth of finance as a set of entirely rational economic practices by showing the significance of emotions in financial markets (Zaloom 2009) and discussing their unpredictability (Appel 2014; Ho 2009b). Studies on gambling, on the other hand, have shown the calculative spirit that people may display in order to make the best bet (Hart 2013: 17; Puri 2015: 466). Moreover, it has been shown that gambling may well be perceived as a form of work and be seen as a job rather than an instance of speculative accumulation (Krige 2011: 5). Taken together, these studies point to the fluidity between the categories of finance and gambling.

The similarities between gambling and finance become even more apparent when we attempt to classify practices that are situated inbetween the common understandings of the two, such as weather trading or spread betting (Loussouarn 2013; Randalls 2013). Pyramid schemes are a particularly interesting example because they are highly controversial economic phenomena and are certainly seen as disreputable and illegitimate by many people. Participants are mostly nonprofessionals, i.e. people who have not received an education in economics and have little or no experience with complicated financial products and transactions. Although they pay money into the scheme in the hope to get rich quickly, pyramid scheme participants do not understand their activity to be gambling, instead seeing it as work. Indeed, the profitability of their investment depends on their success in recruiting further participants which they conceive of as their job. They go about their activities not in demarcated zones of gambling such as race courses or casinos, but in office spaces. Moreover, participants are striving to become professional businesspeople. They begin dressing like businesspeople, thinking like businesspeople and acting like businesspeople. Some of them do so quite successfully and indeed professionalize in their field, which may increase their reputation among colleagues and enable them to increase their profits.

Despite the structural similarity of pyramid schemes and MLM, the latter is recognized as a reasonable form of business in most legislative systems. The distinction between MLM and pyramid schemes is mainly made along the lines of the product. MLM is legal because the marketing scheme involves products, whereas pyramid schemes are illegal because there is no product or a fake product. However, the significance of products in MLM is often secondary. Without the system of belief that the companies construct around the products, these would be much less marketable. MLM developed out of door-to-door salesmanship, which traditionally distributed household appliances and personal care items directly to the customer. The industry changed significantly around the mid twentieth century when a multiple levels sales structure was introduced that encouraged salespeople to recruit further salespeople (Biggart 1989). As the recruiters were remunerated for the sales of their recruits, this allowed for the possibility of making money without actually selling things. Moreover, it encouraged the imagination of significant wealth. As the efforts of many salespeople shifted from selling to recruitment, the products retreated into the background. It would be reductionist to describe MLM simply as a particular form of retail. The companies have elaborate systems of compensation and bonus payments that are designed to create the impression that people can easily become rich. The fact that the industry appears to be selling mainly to its own distributors is a telling point (Keep and Vander Nat 2014: 204).

The comparison of MLM and pyramid schemes that I present in this work is revealing because it shows the grey zone between business and gambling and the fine line between legitimate and illegitimate economic activity. Moreover, it provides insights into the dynamics through which these two pyramidal structures relate to one another.

Capitalist Magic

Instead of seeing capitalism, and finance in particular, as an economic system of rationality, we may as well depart from the assumption that it is just the opposite: a system relying on myth making and enchantment. Arjun Appadurai (2012), for example, argues that a new form of magical thinking permeates financial markets. Departing from Weber, Appadurai calls for the necessity to identify the spirit of contemporary capitalism. We should not assume that capitalism is a self-perpetuating force set off by an initial ethical moment as identified by Weber. Today, Appadurai suggests, at the heart of capitalism are a number of magical practices that are based on faith in the market. Techniques of predicting the future, such as financial charts, aim at making an uncertain future knowable. They treat the market as a source of certainty and scientific rationality, but may be compared with the charts of astronomers or tarot card operators. Similarly, Laura Bear (2015) compares capitalist speculation to divination. Capitalist action, she argues, could be seen as 'motivated by forms of augury that make visible invisible forces and promise to draw humans closer to knowledge of the hidden patterns of society and the universe' (2015: 410). She suggests that bureaucrat-speculators' practices of calculating probabilities and risk may well be seen as forms of magic.

These ideas are interesting in relation to the fact that the proliferation of MLM and pyramid schemes depends upon successfully converting people to the belief system they construct, for example, through elaborate systems of profit calculation. The belief system is secular, but, as I will show in Chapter 3, they are economic structures that bear striking similarities to religious movements. In order to succeed, MLM and pyramid schemes have to convince people that there is a stable business behind their activities that consists in the circulation of valuable products or meaningful services. They try to avoid the idea of speculative enterprise that channels money from the pockets of the many to those of a few.

Peter Cahn (2011) shows convincingly in his ethnography of MLM in Mexico that involvement means more to people than an attempt to make money. Positive thinking philosophy is an important part of the business and their participation may be of significant spiritual significance for the distributors. The formation of the self, according to the principles set by the companies, is a key element in MLM. This includes both the cultivation of the body through the consumption of products and the cultivation of the mind through the strength of positive thought and belief in a better future. The spiritual significance of both MLM and pyramid schemes in the postsocialist context and the magical qualities that are attributed to products and services will be discussed in Chapters 3 and 5 respectively.

Appearance and myth making are important in a further sense in MLM and pyramid schemes. It has been argued that drama is key to speculative enterprise (Tsing 2005). Tsing shows this by discussing the example of a Canadian company that was responsible for a major gold mining scandal in the Indonesian rainforest. Only through charismatic performance and the conjuring of mystery could the company successfully attract international finance capital. Tsing's study presents an interesting parallel to my findings because drama and performance are absolutely essential for the proliferation of MLM and pyramid schemes. However, in the case of MLM and pyramid schemes, we are dealing with drama in a very literal sense. The companies rent venues with stages for their performances, often theatres or music halls. Charismatic leaders try to enchant their audience with their personal rags-to-riches stories and to lead them into dream worlds by showing them films of their luxury holidays, houses, cars and swimming pools. Their conclusion is always the same: everyone can be successful if they only firmly believe that their dreams can become true. Belief is built upon a particular construction of the future. Possibility is emphasized, whereas probability is neglected. The possibility that everyone could be the one who makes a profit is the key narrative, while the reality that only very few people make a profit thanks to the failure of many others is a taboo topic.

This study seeks to illuminate the techniques companies use in order to instil belief in MLM and pyramid schemes. It is these techniques that account for the similarities of the schemes across the globe. Each scheme is of course also embedded in particular social contexts and throughout this book I will take into account how they resonate within specific cultural environments and social structures. I am interested to see how the companies are able to construct and sustain the illusion that their activities are beneficial in the face of significant evidence to the contrary. An investigation of this question will further question capitalism as a system of economic rationality and will help us to better understand its appeal around the globe.

Method

When I arrived in Aga in July 2014, I knew that MLM was popular in the district. As I have described above, I had been invited into an Amway office during my first short fieldwork stay in 2011 and was fascinated by the performance of an enthusiastic Amway distributor who wanted to recruit me. When I began hearing about other schemes, I became truly curious about the whole matter and decided to take the ethnographic puzzle of the pyramid boom in Aga as a point of departure for a research project.

A few days after my arrival in 2014, I met a friend with whom I had been in touch since 2011 and chatted with him about my research interest. When he heard that I intended to study the MLM industry, his first idea was that I should start a scheme myself. He was absolutely convinced that I could make a great profit because people would believe me if I told them that they could make a lot of money from my scheme. They would believe me, he said, because I was from Germany.

I did not start a scheme and also I decided not to register with any of the companies. This was difficult because I was seen to be an ideal recruit. When I met the *seteviki*,[7] the people who were actively pushing the schemes, their first reaction was that I could join their network and then start selling and advertising in Germany, a wealthy country where the schemes would then proliferate to their benefit. This idea of interconnectedness with an economically powerful place excited them. My explanation that I had come in order to study the schemes and not to do business was rarely accepted. The *seteviki* were used to hearing and ignoring excuses for refusal to become involved. Many of them continued to hope until the end of my research that they could convince me to study the schemes *and* do business with them.

There were several reasons for my decision not to become involved. Importantly, I could study the schemes without so doing. I was welcome to spend time in the companies' offices, to participate in the seminars (even those for the schemes' participants only), I was given insight into the materials they were using for training purposes, and *seteviki* talked to me and gave me interviews. If I had agreed to register, I would have been pushed to recruit or sell, both of which I saw as ethically problematic. Even if I had only registered, I am quite sure that they would have used this formal act as an advertisement to lend authority to their activity – again placing me in an ethically unacceptable situation. Finally, my involvement might have seriously damaged my reputation as a researcher and my relationships with informants who were not involved in the schemes.

I did my research largely in the town of Aginskoe. Occasionally, however, I went to cities in order to participate in company events, or other towns and villages in order to meet informants. While I investigated all of the schemes I encountered, I put a particular focus on one MLM company, Amway, and on one pyramid scheme, WIC Holding. These were the companies that were most active during the time of my research and the representatives of both companies were particularly interested to speak to me and willing to answer my questions. Hence, many, but not all, of the examples in this book refer to these two companies.

My research at times put me in ethically difficult positions. I relied on the *seteviki* for information and they helped me a lot, were very friendly and were willing to support my research. The trouble was that I found their activities to be highly problematic. In general I did not comment on what they were doing unless I was asked for my opinion. This did not happen very often, but when they asked, I gave an honest answer. I did not do anything to actively hinder their business (which would have made my research impossible), but I spoke to many people about my findings and about the problems associated with the schemes.

The schemes provided a revealing lens through which to look at the local economy. Economic difficulties and hopes were frequently discussed in the offices and meetings by those who were thinking about joining and those who were already involved. These discussions revealed much about the ways in which people think about the economy, about logics that steer economic action, and about ideas of cooperation, loyalty and trust. MLM and pyramid schemes entail new and interesting forms of social interaction because they introduce new forms of economic reasoning. The ways in which people engage with them, understand them and negotiate them reflect and reveal social processes and cultural logics that are significant beyond the realm of the schemes themselves.

In order to understand how the schemes are embedded in the wider economic context, I spoke to people about money making, debts, credit, job markets, banks, insurance, prices and business. I had the impression that people enjoyed talking about these topics because they were linked to questions that troubled or excited them. Often it was not me who brought up such issues; rather, my informants chose these topics of conversation. The economy was a salient issue in part because of the economic crisis triggered by the fall in oil prices as well as the sanctions imposed on Russia following Russia's annexation of Crimea and its military intervention in Ukraine, which dominated news reports throughout the time of my research. While I was in Russia, the crisis slowly began to be felt through a rise in prices, delays in wage payments, the fall in the value of the rouble and budget cuts in several public institutions. People's interest in discussing questions concerning livelihood strategies was intensified as a result of the unstable economic situation in the present, the uncertainty with regard to the future and the memory of the dramatic economic changes after socialism. Apart from discussing these matters with informants, I visited acquaintances at their workplaces, in shops, markets, banks, public institutions and offices, went shopping with them, accompanied them to banks, and observed economic exchange and negotiations at the household level. Moreover, perhaps rather unusually for an anthropologist undertaking field research, I rented a small office in Aginskoe, next to one of the offices from where a pyramid scheme was operated. At first, this was merely for practical reasons, such as to have a warm place where I could spend time between events or meetings with people and a quiet place where I could write my field diary and invite people for interviews or conversations. However, my office turned out to be a very valuable research tool. Not only did it allow me to closely observe what was going on in the office next door and to build close relations with the people who were working and visiting there, but it also provided a space where people knew they could find me. I had some of the best and most insightful conversations with people who came to my office when *they* wanted to talk to me or to get to know me. Rather than limiting contact to situations when I would seek out people in order to speak to them, the office allowed for more mutuality between me and my informants.

A particularly valuable source of data was the household where I lived throughout the time of my research. I stayed with a Buryat family whom I had known for several years before I started the research, which this book is based upon. Living with them in their small wooden house in a village adjacent to the town of Aginskoe, I had the opportunity to participate in the everyday life of the family, to celebrate holidays with them and to get to know many of their relatives and acquaintances. I could observe their household coping strategies and their practices of sharing, exchange and mutual support. My observations constantly raised new questions that I could then investigate with regard to other households and discuss with further informants.

During my research, I interacted mainly with Buryats and got to know very few Russians. This was not intentional, nor was it entirely coincidental. My first acquaintances in the field were Buryats and some of my most important informants I met through their almost exclusively Buryat friends and relatives. Furthermore, although a third of Aginskoe's population is Russian, Russians are largely absent from public life in the town. Regardless of which event I attended, there were rarely any Russians present. Most notable is the fact that virtually no Russians were actively involved in the companies that were the focus of my research. This is a particularity of MLM and pyramid schemes in Aga, but is certainly not true for Russia in general. In the cities where I attended seminars, there were predominantly Russian *seteviki*. However, as I spent most of my time in the town of Aginskoe, I conducted my research largely among Buryats. Nevertheless, many of my observations and conclusions may well be applicable to Russians and where I found ethnicity to be relevant, I make this explicit.

I conducted my research in the Russian language, which I know fluently. My knowledge of Buryat remained very limited throughout my fieldwork and although I could understand its basic vocabulary, I was not able to use the language actively. I did not have the impression that language issues restricted my data collection to a significant degree. First, in many instances Buryats speak Russian, especially when talking about economic matters such as MLM and pyramid schemes or use a mix of Buryat and Russian, which I understand fairly well. Second, when speaking to me directly or giving interviews, people always used the Russian language. Sometimes, when only Buryat was spoken, Buryat friends translated for me. This, however, did not occur very often because in group situations, there were usually also Buryats who had only a poor knowledge of Buryat, meaning that Russian was used predominantly.

Hugely beneficial for my ability to access data was the fact that people were very curious about me simply because I came from the West. They found it amusing that I had decided to come to this 'cold middle of nowhere' (their words!) in order to do research. People liked the idea that I would write about Aga: they were supportive of my search for information and they were very keen to leave me with a good impression. For this reason, I felt that some people were somewhat disappointed that I had come to study MLM and pyramid schemes instead of their beautiful songs, dances or religious traditions. The authorities were also supportive of my research. They answered the questions that interested me and I had no problems in gaining access to the town's archive, newspaper archives and statistical information.

Outline of the Book

Each chapter of this book approaches MLM and pyramid schemes from a different angle. Taken together, they cover the themes that have emerged from my fieldwork as most relevant with regard to broader questions within economic anthropology and they are built on examples of sites and interactions that I have found to be important across schemes. I decided not to discuss MLM and pyramid schemes in separate chapters as their histories in Aga are closely intertwined and in many instances the same people were involved in both types of schemes. It is necessary to differentiate between them and I will do so throughout the book. Overall, however, I think it is of greater analytical value to highlight their similarities rather than trying to set clear boundaries. I therefore draw on examples from both MLM and pyramid schemes to support my arguments.

The first chapter, which follows this introduction, traces Aga's economic development from the end of socialism until the time of my research, dealing with the severe economic crisis of the 1990s, the district's economic miracle achieved through its special economic zone status, and the relatively recent problem of severe household indebtedness. The chapter is concerned with the particular ways in which capitalism unfolds locally. It shows how market rationalities are embedded within a dense system of informal support that characterizes Aga's economy and how the logics of mutual support determine economic decision making and flows of money.

The second chapter serves to provide a deeper understanding of the nature of MLM and pyramid schemes by investigating their history and structure. Here, I discuss similarities and differences in order to clarify the relationship between a globally applied marketing model and an investment scam. Moreover, this chapter will give a first idea of how MLM and pyramid schemes manifest locally, who is pushing them and how people think about them. Chapters 1 and 2 aim at providing the background information for the discussions of the subsequent chapters.

Chapter 3 discusses MLM and pyramid schemes as forms of 'spiritual capitalism' that bear striking similarities with religious movements. The chapter argues that the appeal of MLM and pyramid schemes needs to be seen within the context of the surge of new religious and spiritual movements after socialism, all offering people new forms of hope. A more detailed picture of a MLM company, Amway, and a pyramid scheme, WIC Holding, is given with the purpose of revealing the techniques through which they attract participants and build communities.

In the fourth chapter, I zoom in on the microsocial environments within which MLM and pyramid schemes operate. The focus is on kinship relations and their role for the proliferation of the schemes. The importance of kinship will be shown with regard to the strategies used to push the schemes, the dynamics that the schemes develop and the consequences of their collapse. What I wish to demonstrate in this chapter is both how social organization constitutes pathways for economic action and how social patterns are integrated into new economic realities. I argue that kinship relations have not lost their significance under capitalism, but rather that it is kinship that sets the frame for the development of commerce, conditioning economic decision making and channelling flows of money. In the cases of MLM and pyramid schemes, the social mechanisms of obligation, trust and solidarity work in the interest of the companies and, because most people fail, have problematic effects on the whole community.

Chapter 5 scrutinizes the significance of the goods and services marketed through MLM and pyramid schemes. Here I explore the question of how commodity value is constituted within various local contexts of economic reasoning. The chapter analyses the appeal of the products within the formerly socialist rural market, explores the role of consumption for the cultivation of social and informal economic relations, and looks at the symbolic and emotional values that become attached to the products through the systemic logic of the schemes. Extending the arguments of previous chapters, I contend that in many instances, the purchase of the schemes' goods or services cannot be understood in terms of individual cost/benefit considerations. Consumption must be seen as embedded within the local economy of support and as tied to hopes of prosperity and aspirations to become successful businesspeople.

Chapter 6 deals with the corporate culture and internal power dynamics of MLM and pyramid schemes. It explores the mechanisms through which companies discipline their workforces and enhance their loyalty. I look at the ways in which participants grow into their jobs, how they learn the techniques of marketing and how they internalize the industry's morality. The chapter shows that it is not only a system of incentives that encourages people to act in the companies' interest; rather, direct forms of pressure through internal hierarchies alongside systemic pressure stemming from corporate organization play a crucial role in this regard.

While the preceding chapters investigate the local manifestation of MLM and pyramid schemes, the conclusion of this book zooms out of Siberia and looks at the schemes in the context of broader economic trends. It argues that an analysis of MLM and pyramid schemes reveals problems of the capitalist system at large. By comparing MLM to the 'gig economy' and elaborating on the idea of pyramid schemes as a response to finance capitalism, the problematic nature of working conditions and economic rights in our neoliberal era is highlighted.

Notes

1. Ponzi schemes are often confused with pyramid schemes. In both pyramid and Ponzi schemes, existing investors are financially compensated from the contributions made by new investors. But while investors in Ponzi schemes are (misleadingly) informed that they are earning returns simply from their investments, participants in pyramid schemes are usually aware that their income is dependent on the recruitment of new investors and that they themselves must recruit additional investors, who will themselves recruit new investors, and so on. This may at first sight seem an insignificant detail, but in fact it is important because the multilevel structure resulting from the recruitment strategy of many pyramid schemes makes them virtually indistinguishable from MLM. I will elaborate on this difference in Chapter 2.
2. There is another Buryat region outside Buryatia, the Ust-Orda district, which also had autonomous status until it became part of Irkutsk Oblast in 2008.
3. See the website of the Aga district's administration (Administratsiia Aginskogo Buriatskogo Okruga): http://www.aginskoe.ru/node/32.

4. There is no separate statistical data for the ethnic composition of the town (only for the district). It is said that the share of Buryats is higher in Aginskoe than in the district as a whole and the percentages given are estimations of the head of the statistical authority in Aginskoe. The data about the ethnic composition of the district is problematic because there are a considerable number of people with parents of different ethnic background.
5. A total of 286 families left the Aginsk aimak with large numbers of cattle between September 1923 and October 1924 (Tumunov 1993: 39).
6. In 2011, 929 people left the district, while in 2012, out-migration numbered 1,146 people (Zabaikalkraistat 2013).
7. The adjective *setevoi* means 'network', so *seteviki* could be translated as 'networkers'. This is the term by which active participants in the *setevoi biznes* (network business or network marketing) refer to themselves. Participants in both MLM and pyramid schemes use it as a generic title for their jobs. When I write about the group of people who actively push MLM and/or pyramid schemes and who see their involvement as their profession, I will use the term *seteviki*. When referring to MLM salespeople only, I will use the term 'distributors', as this is most common in the literature on the topic. Distributors and pyramid scheme participants may or may not see their involvement in MLM and pyramid schemes respectively as a profession. This will be discussed in detail in Chapter 2.

1

CAPITALISM IN AGA

With the demise of the Soviet Union, the last significant bulwark against global capitalism collapsed. The West saw itself as the winner of the Cold War and the ideology of the free market was able to expand into new territory. As the states that had been part of the Soviet Bloc sank into a deep economic crisis, they were immediately offered the remedy of neoliberal doctrine: shock therapy was to guarantee a quick and smooth transition to a capitalist market economy. Supported by the IMF and the World Bank, privatization was initiated, state subsidies were cut, free trade was introduced and prices were liberalized.

As a number of anthropological studies of postsocialist societies have shown, shock therapy largely failed to achieve what it promised. In many places, particularly in rural regions, its effects were far from what economic theory predicted and market liberalization disadvantaged many people (Humphrey 1999; Humphrey and Mandel 2002; Sneath 2012; Verdery 2003; Woodruff 1999). All these studies draw attention to the fact that shock therapy was not implemented on a *tabula rasa*. The past could not simply be erased overnight and be replaced by a functioning market. Instead, there were particular economic moralities and practices in place that determined and shaped the sort of capitalism that developed.

This chapter is an account of how the onset of the capitalist era was experienced in Aga, tracing economic development in the district after the end of socialism. My account is necessarily sketchy because it covers nearly a quarter of a century. Many of the issues raised could be discussed in greater detail, but the objective here is to convey a basic idea of how capitalism as a set of practices, as well as an idea, unfolded within and in response to the given context. The chapter serves to provide the background information needed in order to understand the logics and the appeal of MLM and pyramid schemes in Aga. In the first part of the chapter, I focus on the possibilities of making a livelihood in the new market environment and on the economic difficulties people are experiencing, in particular in the face of debt. The second part of the chapter will be devoted to nonmarket forms of giving and exchange that are often based on the logic of mutual support. As I will then show, market and nonmarket economic activities and rationalities do not simply coexist as parallel systems, but frequently crosscut and intermingle. I argue that informal economic activity, which was crucial to circumventing the shortcomings of the socialist planned economy, has not lost its significance. Instead, it has adapted to new economic realities and plays a crucial role in dealing with the challenges of the capitalist economy.

Aga's Economy after Socialism

The economic crisis that followed the demise of the Soviet Union was devastating especially in rural regions (Burawoy 1999; Humphrey 1998; Verdery 2003). With a GDP reaching only 31 per cent of the Russian average in 2003, the situation in Aga was particularly precarious (Nezavisimyi Institut Sotsial'noi Politiki 2004). The area of today's Zabaykalsky Krai had been an important military zone during Soviet times and the military infrastructure had played an enormous role in the region's development. With the dismantling of the military zone in the 1990s, the region became one of the poorest parts of Russia. The enterprises that had catered for the military infrastructure collapsed and the most important market for agricultural products was lost (Nezavisimyi Institut Sotsial'noi Politiki 2004). Moreover, state subsidies, which had been crucial for the operation of collective farms, were cut. Without state support, the privatized farms could barely make a profit in a liberalized market (cf. Humphrey and Sneath 1999: 78–90). As the collective farms could no longer pay wages, it became difficult to make a living in the countryside. In the search for alternatives, many people left their villages in order to look for employment in towns or cities. The population of the district centre, Aginskoe, grew significantly during this time due to the influx of villagers.

Life in Aga in the 1990s was a struggle. With the dismantling of the planned economy, a large number of jobs were lost, not just temporarily but irretrievably. These included jobs on collective farms such as tractor-drivers, milkers or shepherds, jobs in the administration and management of collective farms and in the district centres, and jobs in educational institutions that had prepared youth for specialized professions in the agricultural sector. The rate of unemployment was high and those who had a job were paid only irregularly. There was a time, one of my informants remembered, when teachers had not received their wages for eight months and children sat in the schools in hats and winter coats because there was no money for heating. The social privileges of the Soviet system were gone and what the people had received free of charge before, most notably medication and education, now had to be paid for. As neither institutions nor the people had money, a 'barter-and-subsistence economy' developed during this period (Humphrey 1999: 20). People survived on potatoes and cabbage harvested in their yards and on meat and milk products from their cattle. Those who were desperate enough went 'to the trains' (*na vagony*). This meant going to Moguitui, a small town with the only train station in Aga. Moguitui was a stop for freight trains going from China to the west of Russia at that time. When a train came to halt, one person broke open a wagon and the horde of people who had come 'to the train' stormed the wagon and grabbed as much of the freight as they could get hold of. People hoped to be able to trade the goods for other things they needed. Raiding the trains involved risking their lives because the guards watching the trains stood ready to shoot at them. The 1990s were an economically destitute decade in this part of Russia and in rural regions many men (and smaller numbers of women) found comfort only in alcohol.

One of the few possibilities to make money during the economic crisis of the 1990s was to engage in trade. As private trade had been illegal during Soviet times, this was something people felt uncomfortable about at first. However, the circumstances left no alternative. Some people grew cabbage for sale in Chita and others brought newspapers, groceries or alcohol from the city to earn a few roubles by selling the goods at a slightly higher price in the district. Due to the geographical closeness to the Chinese border, crossborder trade began to flourish. It became profitable to travel 300 kilometres to Manzhouli, the Chinese border town in order to import cheap low-quality clothes and household items for sale in the improvised market in Aginskoe's town centre. The high demand for affordable Chinese consumer goods fuelled Manzhouli's rise from a small town with a few wooden houses to the glittering consumer paradise that it is today. In contrast, Zabaikalsk, the border town on the Russian side, has remained what it was: a few Soviet concrete blocks surrounded by small houses, a few run-down cafes and tiny shops along the main road and a hard-to-find bus station from which traders and tourists can depart to China.

During the first decade after the end of the socialist era, most people could afford only the most indispensable items. Even if guests came to visit, people remember today, they could offer hardly more than tea, bread and sugar. The glamorous world of capitalism remained distant, confined to the TV screen. The American TV series *Santa Barbara* gained huge popularity during the early 1990s along with a number of Latin-American soap operas. For the first time, people in rural Siberia received nonpoliticized and idealized images of consumerist worlds with alternative lifestyles, fashion and domestic interiors. People were fascinated with these worlds, and the fates of the people inhabiting them were subject of endless discussions. These series contributed greatly to shaping ideas of the world beyond the reality surrounding them.

In the late 1990s, Aga saw an economic miracle that over the following years improved the situation in the district considerably. This was certainly not anticipated at the time and is now looked back upon as a stroke of genius. This is what happened according to Makhachkeev (2007) and to accounts of my informants. Bair Zhamsuev, a local politician who had made a political career in the Komsomol and the Communist Party, was elected as a deputy in the State Duma in 1993. In Moscow, he managed to establish good relations with a number of influential politicians and entrepreneurs. These relations were an important basis for the support of Zhamsuev's policies as head of the district's administration from 1997 until 2008. Having been elected head of the administration, he suggested making the district a special economic zone. Aga's autonomous status facilitated a legal arrangement that allowed the district to create a tax haven and to boost its budget. In order to realize his plan, Zhamsuev needed a strong lobby in Moscow. During his time as a deputy, he had met Iosif Kobzon, a famous Soviet singer and influential politician who is suspected to have sustained ties with the organized crime networks known as the Russian Mafia. As Zhamsuev said in an interview, he had approached Kobzon with the suggestion that he should run as Aga's State Duma Deputy to support the district's interests in Moscow. Kobzon agreed and was elected, and Zhamsuev's strategy proved to be successful. Thanks to Zhamsuev's and Kobzon's contacts, a number of large corporations registered in Aga and began paying taxes in the district. Between 1999 and 2004, Aga's GDP rose significantly and unemployment decreased from 25 per cent in 2002 to less than

10 per cent in 2004. However, despite the economic upswing, wages remained among the lowest in Russia (Nezavisimyi Institut Sotsial'noi Politiki 2004). The local political leadership used the money to promote production, small entrepreneurship and agriculture, and to pave roads, renovate schools and build sports facilities. Those who were in charge at that time remember almost with disbelief that there was a time when they did not know how to spend all the money they were accumulating. Today, there are different opinions on whether best use has been made of the money brought in by the tax haven policy, but Zhamsuev remains a very popular politician because he managed to create these favourable economic conditions and Kobzon, Deputy of the Zabaykalsky Krai since 2008, continues to enjoy his role as the district's patron, using his networks to support the Aga Buryats.

Aga's economic boom years came to an end when the district merged with the much larger Chita Oblast' in 2008 into the territorial-administrative unit of Zabaykalsky Krai. Whereas in the 1990s, Chita had been economically stronger than the small enclave, Aga's economy was clearly better developed by the time of the referendum that was forced upon the district's citizens. The unification was obviously not in their interests, either economically or in terms of ethnonational political representation. Curiously, a majority of people voted for unification. Their decision appears to have been due to pressure from above: public-sector employees report that they had been warned that they might lose their jobs if they voted against unification. This was a serious threat to those with a stable income on which whole families depended, and most complied. Moreover, as Long and Graber point out, people were aware that the unification plans were part of a political process initiated in Moscow. Several administrational units in Russia were amalgamated at that time and people knew that they were not the only victims. Therefore, the majority took a pragmatic stance with their vote, even if they did not enthusiastically support the development. Rather than risking conflict over a matter that they perceived as already lost, people preferred to underline their general support of Russia's national politics (Long and Graber 2009: 151–52).

With the administrative amalgamation, Aga lost its autonomy and, as a consequence, it lost its status as a special economic zone and the monetary blessing came to an end. Six years after the end of the cash injection, Aga still appears to be a little paradise within the territory of the Zabaykalsky Krai. On taking a closer look, however, one can literally see facades crumbling. The development that was initiated during the 'good times' could not be sustained without the influx of tax money from outside. The local court does not even have money to buy envelopes, an employee explained to me in the post office. As a consequence of the economic crisis resulting from EU sanctions against Russia, further cuts in the district's budget were expected during the time of my research.

Aga's industry, consisting of a small number of mining, food processing and timber processing enterprises, is weakly developed and accounts for less than 20 per cent of its revenue.[1] People rely heavily on subsistence-based agriculture and livestock herding, and for the most part only small surpluses of meat, potatoes or cabbage are sold in order to gain some cash for household expenses. It remains very difficult to earn a regular income through farming. In the liberalized market, locally produced milk, for example, cannot compete in price with its mass-produced Tetra Pak rival. There are plans to create new forms of agricultural cooperation to increase the competitiveness of livestock holders as well as plans to promote the processing industry. However, the crisis has postponed the prospect of this happening into the indefinite future. Jobs in the public sector, for example in schools, hospitals or administrative structures, are highly desired in Aga. These jobs are one of the few sources of regular income in the district (the other major source being pensions) and signify financial stability. Despite the fact that about half of the district's population is Russian, the leading positions in state institutions are overwhelmingly occupied by Buryats. Access to these jobs depends much more on kinship networks than on professional qualifications, a fact that restricts the Russian population's access to this job market. Although these public-sector jobs are associated with financial stability, employees complained about delays in the payment of wages (*zaderzhki*), sometimes over the course of several months, during my research in 2011 as well as in 2014–15.

Private small-scale entrepreneurship has developed since the late 1990s and a number of hairdressers, convenience stores, cafes, taxi services, pawn shops, traders and repair services compete for customers. In most cases, the new entrepreneurs have no professional training in their sphere of activity and they work alone or in small teams, often consisting of family members. The situation for many of them is ultimately precarious and uncertain. Their income is unstable and dependent on the financial situation of their family, as well as being highly vulnerable to fluctuations in the national and the global economy. Crossborder trade, for example, is becoming less and less profitable, particularly in light of the drastic drop of the rouble as a consequence of the EU sanctions imposed upon Russia in 2014. Frequently, small enterprises close down, to be replaced by others who run into similar difficulties to their predecessors after some time. A major problem reported by Aga's entrepreneurs is the lack of purchasing power amongst potential customers. People have no money, they say, and their customers have become used to buying everything on credit. Most debtors repay the money when they receive their salary or pension or when they are able to borrow money from someone else. However, there are always those who do not pay their debts. Many traders have cash-flow problems, which lead to difficulties in stocking their stores because they have not been paid for goods already sold. They find pursuing debtors difficult, tiresome and too often unsuccessful.

During the time of my research, I became good friends with a group of young Aga entrepreneurs, all men in their early thirties. Whenever we sat together, they would sooner or later start discussing their ideas for new business projects. They were all struggling to earn a livelihood and therefore they were constantly concerned with how to make the most money in Aginskoe. Aldar,[2] who worked as a private moneylender, considered opening a hair salon as he found it increasingly difficult and frustrating to recover debts from his customers. When I left Aginskoe after my fieldwork, he was still trying to find money to buy the basic equipment for his new business. Baatar had a repair service for electronic devices, but had to give it up in the spring of 2015 because he had not paid the rent for his shop for six months. He started operating a taxi service instead and worked as a driver himself. Amgalan also ran a repair service. He enjoyed speaking about advertising and considered himself to be an expert in this regard. And, indeed, as the first and only entrepreneur in town, he had a neon sign installed in his shop window. Amgalan, like Aldar and Baatar, was always seeking the most profitable business opportunities. During the time of my research, he decided that in a place where nobody had money, this would be a pawn shop. Shortly before I left, he had finally managed to overcome all the bureaucratic obstacles and opened the pawn shop next to his repair service.

Money always seems to be scarce in Aga, even for those who have jobs. People constantly refer to a lack of money. The general tenor of their remarks is that they have enough to cope, but not enough to live. Money to buy bread can always be found, but people cannot earn enough to finance the lifestyle they desire. Wages and pensions are low in Aga and state benefits are a symbolic rather than a practical support.[3] The registered number of unemployed people is low only in official statistics, which is easily explained by the fact that people have no motivation to register themselves as unemployed.[4] The procedure of registration is a bureaucratic nightmare and the subsidies one may receive are so insignificant that it makes more sense to spend the time earning small sums by chopping wood, working as an unlicensed taxi driver or as a transport worker at the Russian–Chinese border. In the light of the scarcity of money, subsistence farming continues to be highly significant as a source of a stable food supply for households.

Debt in Aga

People in Aga who grew up during the socialist era are nostalgic about the times when money did not particularly trouble them. What they needed was either inexpensive in relation to their salaries or it was free. This perception is unsurprising, given the restricted function of money in the Soviet planned economy in comparison to today's capitalist economy (Rona-Tas and Guseva 2014). In Soviet times, the state provided a number of free services such as education and healthcare, along with maternity and disability leave, and subsidized housing and vacations. Moreover, desired consumer goods were rationed and it was mostly a question of access rather than of money as to whether they could be purchased. Informal social networks were crucial to getting information about where and when television sets, refrigerators or cars would be sold or to obtain certain consumer goods underhand. For these reasons, possession of money was often not the most significant factor in terms of whether people could access their desires (Rona-Tas and Guseva: 31-44). With the demise of the Soviet Union and the retreat of the welfare state, money immediately became an object of scarcity. It became difficult to earn and was not only needed for necessities, but was also desired for the attractive new consumer goods that swept on to the postsocialist market.

Before *Perestroika*, financial operations at the household level were minimal.[5] There was a single state bank that regulated monetary operations and financial transactions. The bank offered citizens a savings account in which they could deposit their money. Wages were paid in cash and payments at the household level were also made in cash (Curtis 1996). Thus, money was a very visible and tangible means of exchange. For larger purchases such as a refrigerator, a motorbike or furniture, consumer credit was available. As high rates of interest were seen to be immoral and detrimental to the consumer, rates of interest were regulated and very low (Prokhorov 1973).[6] Moreover, payments were often deducted directly from wages. Therefore, borrowing was largely devoid of risk (Rona-Tas and Guseva 2014: 33).

The transition from the socialist economy to a capitalist economy included a major restructuring of the banking sector. A two-tier system with one central bank and numerous commercial banks was established, following the standard model in market economies. Initially, the regulation of commercial banking in Russia was lax in comparison to other postsocialist countries. This led to a mushrooming of unstable commercial banks during the 1990s, many of which went bankrupt after short periods of operation (Rona-Tas and Guseva 2014: 34–41).

It was shortly after the turn of the millennium that the bank 'Russkii Standart' first began to offer consumer credits. The bank signed contracts with large retail chains that enabled customers to buy consumer goods on credit directly in the store. Other banks were quick to follow and a large consumer credit market developed in Russia (Vasil'eva 2011). Today, consumer debt has reached alarming heights in the country. In 2013, the IMF warned Russia regarding its increasing household debt burden. Unsecured loans on consumer purchases were growing at a rate up to 60 per cent. Loan growth in banks has outpaced deposits, which the IMF evaluated as being a threat to the financial stability of banks (Dyakina 2013).

Apart from problems at the macroeconomic level, the situation has become increasingly difficult for debtors struggling to pay back their loans. Legislation sets no limits on rates of interest, which have reached exploitative levels of up to 50 per cent, and debt-collection practices are unregulated (Raksina 2013). A law allowing for personal bankruptcy only came into force in October 2015. Insufficient consumer protection has led to desperate financial situations and personal tragedies, in particular in regions where the need for money is great. Unscrupulous banks were able to take advantage of the fact that most people had little experience with monetary operations and recognized the true costs of consumer loans only when they were already heavily indebted (Egorov 2015).

Southeastern Siberia is among the Russian regions with the greatest household indebtedness in relation to the gross regional product (Rudenko and Volkova 2013). There are no separate statistics for Aga, but during my research, debt was a permanent concern for nearly all my informants. Debt is perceived as a severe problem and is constantly discussed. Many find themselves in the desperate situation that all the money they earn is immediately lost to the banks. In order to manage debt, it has become normal practice to take out credits in order to pay creditors. Those who are heavily indebted know that they will never be able to earn enough money in Aga or in the nearby cities in order to free themselves from debt. There is much talk about going to Magadan in the Russian north for a couple of years, where temperatures are low and wages are high. No one likes the idea of living there, far from their home and their families, but people do not see any alternative in order to escape the vicious circle of debt.

The debt misery in Aga is a relatively recent development. After the 2008 economic crisis and in the course of an economic upswing in the country, banks simplified the procedure for taking out loans. Banks granted consumer credit to almost everyone asking for it, and it became common practice to borrow money, partly out of need to cover medical costs or pay for a child's education and partly because of the desire to purchase consumer items. Today, the money business is flourishing in Aga. Credits are offered not only by banks but also by microfinancial institutions that advertise their services everywhere in town, offering 'quick money', 'money in 15 minutes' or 'money before payday'. These microfinancial institutions ask for even higher rates of interest than the banks (around 2 per cent per day), but they provide the money immediately and there is no need for collateral. People make use of their services when they need money urgently and have been unable to borrow from family and friends, which has become increasingly difficult as everyone is struggling to pay back their own debts.

The situation in Aga can be compared to the Mongolian case in which the household debt burden is also a serious problem. Credit schemes for pastoralists were intended to be used for investment, but were in fact spent on necessities. As a result, people are increasingly unable to pay back their loans and the regime of debt contributes significantly to the impoverishment of the countryside (Sneath 2012). The Russian case reveals the power of banking interests even more clearly, as the consumer credit was not even intended to be for investment and one may assume that it was entirely foreseeable that, given the high rates of interest, it would cause immense problems of repayment and great profits for the banks in the long run. This only underlines Sneath's (2012) argument that neoliberal reforms had devastating consequences for those in the greatest need of money and clearly reveals the problematic side of a loosely regulated financial market.

Aga's Economy of Support

In Aga, new ways of reasoning required by the capitalist economy mingle with older regimes of ideas and practices that defined economic relations during socialism and in pre-revolutionary times. A key mechanism of Aga's economy is an informal system of support that steers material flows and labour. I will argue that the logics of this system are rooted both in local morality and in the socialist economy. It is important to emphasize that this logic of support does not exist in parallel to the logic inherent in market transactions, but is closely intertwined with them – it regulates the job market, guides consumer decisions and determines flows of money. The distinction between the realm of the market and the realm of the nonmarket is useful for analytical purposes only. In practice, as has been widely demonstrated in the anthropological literature, these realms are inseparable. This intertwining has been shown most convincingly by scholars who have collapsed the dualism between gift and commodity (Appadurai 1986; Gell 1992; Miller 2001; Sahlins 1972) and demonstrated the market's embeddedness in society (Granovetter 1985; Gudeman 2008; Zelizer 2005). The particular guise of capitalism in Aga, as I aim to show in the following, is defined by the intermingling of local economic regimes with market logics.

Mutual economic support is extremely important in Buryat society. From their earliest years, children are taught the strong moral imperative to help (*pomogat'*) one another. The readiness to help others is thought to be the basis for being a good person. Frequently, my informants highlighted how they had helped others or referred to acts of support they had received in order to describe their own or other people's qualities. While the moral imperative to help is particularly pronounced within kinship relations, it is not confined to them; it extends to friends, neighbours and other close social relations. The willingness to help one another may depend on the formal and/or emotional strength of their relationship. Acts of support may include material as well as immaterial forms of assistance. It could consist in helping a friend repair his or her car, doing household tasks for one's grandfather, giving money to a younger brother, lending a tractor to a neighbour, harvesting hay for an uncle or herding cattle for relatives who live in the city. Support is expected of people one is close to whenever someone is in the situation to provide it. The flows of goods and assistance may, in this context, best be understood as what David Sneath (2006), drawing on data from Mongolia, describes as 'enactions'. These are flows of goods and assistance that are so natural that they can be seen as materializations of social relations. In contrast to 'transactions', these acts of support are better described in the language of obligation than through the idiom of exchange. Mutual support bears more than economic significance; it is an important basis for the cultivation of social relations in Buryat society. Notably, social interaction often takes place precisely on occasions when people help one another. This is certainly a further reason why people, in general, are inclined to help. Anyone who totally withdrew from supporting others economically would find themselves a social outsider.

While mutual support was already crucial in pre-Soviet times (cf. Linkhovoin 2012: 219; for the Mongolian case, cf. Humphrey and Sneath 1999: 141–47), a more particular type of support emerged during socialism. A characteristic of many socialist and formerly socialist societies is the significance of personal social networks in getting things done (Ledeneva 1998; Pedersen 2007; Yang 1994). With regard to Russia, this phenomenon has been described as an 'economy of favours' (Ledeneva 1998). The Russian term *blat* denotes 'the use of personal networks and informal contacts to obtain goods and services in short supply and to find a way around formal procedures' (Ledeneva 1998: 1). According to Ledeneva, *blat* is a way of acting that developed out of the structural constraints of the socialist economy of shortage and was a crucial means to cope with Soviet realities. Personal networks were important to solve everyday problems, to arrange jobs and to gain access to desired commodities, to housing or to travel. *Blat* comprised practices that were usually framed in terms of mutual help and differed from corruption because they were based on long-term reciprocal relationships and were not compensated by money. According to Ledeneva, *blat* has not disappeared within the capitalist economy, but favours have become reoriented around money, as it is money that is always in 'shortage' in postsocialist society. Focusing on the sphere of new private entrepreneurship, Ledeneva argues that *blat* has lost the everyday significance that it had in Soviet times, but that it is still used to make life easier and more comfortable.

In Aga, people frequently emphasize the significance of social ties in getting things done quickly, inexpensively, confidently or reliably. The term *blat* is not only used among those who grew up in Soviet times, but also among younger generations in order to account for the advantages that may be achieved through good connections. In many cases, a favour may be granted through the sphere of influence people have at their place of work. Teachers can arrange for certain children to be admitted to their school, nurses can provide their relatives with access to favourable treatment in the hospital, and bank employees can influence the conditions under which their acquaintances take out a loan. In both the public and the commercial sectors, favours determine to a significant degree how matters are dealt with and how problems are solved. A crucial basis for acting through favours is the social consensus that personal loyalties rank higher than institutional loyalties.

The strong moral imperative to provide support paired with particular patterns of support that emerged under socialism account for a dense network of assistance that regulates the flow of resources and labour in Aga. Below, I will discuss how this system works in a market environment and the role that money plays in it.

Money and the Economy of Support

In today's capitalist economy, money has come to play an important role within informal social networks. Social relations are often decisive in terms of regulating how money is accessed, channelled, shared and saved. A favour can provide access to a free service, such as a medical check-up, that would otherwise have to be paid for or it may relieve a person from fines, for example, if he or she exceeded the speed limit. Support might take the form of voluntary labour, such as helping someone to build a house, or it may consist in giving someone access to money by arranging a job for this person. Moreover, helping out others by giving or lending money are forms of support that are frequently requested. All of these acts of support are of particular significance in an environment where people need to either get things done without money or to gain access to money in order to get things done. Whereas in socialist times, workplace resources could be used in order to support others through favours, today someone down the line has to pay for them.

Let me offer an example of how money is circulated within such systems of support. Ochirma works as a teacher in Aginskoe. Like other teachers, she had not received her wages for three months due to a budgetary crisis at the time of my research. Unlike other teachers, she was able to cope during this period, incurring only small debts, because she was living with her parents who supported her. However, Ochirma was faced with a dilemma when the school announced that she should accompany a class to an event in Moscow. The school would pay for the train ticket and accommodation, but not for any other expenses. Ochirma knew that she would need several thousand roubles for the journey. She discussed the matter with her mother, who told her that she had no money to lend, but suggested that she should ask her brother. Ochirma, as she told me later, was reluctant to do this because her brother had two small children and was already heavily indebted. Her mother then suggested that she ask a cousin with whom they entertain a very close relationship. Ochirma reminded her mother that her cousin was also a teacher and, just like herself, was in financial trouble at the time. They sat quietly for a while thinking about who else they could ask for help. Then Ochirma's mother suddenly remembered that her niece should have received a few thousand roubles for electricity around this time, a state benefit for teachers living in villages and small towns. With this money, her niece would have to pay her electricity bills. As Ochirma's mother worked for the utility-provider, she has some influence on how matters were dealt with in their office. She called the cousin and suggested that she give the money she had received for electricity to Ochirma. She herself would initiate the necessary arrangements to allow for a delay in payment of the bills. Ochirma would return the money as soon as she received her next salary and then the cousin could pay the bills. The cousin did not seem to be enthusiastic about the idea, but she agreed and thus the matter was resolved. This case shows how kinship obligation overlaps with *blat* and it demonstrates the importance of mutual support in dealing with monetary scarcity. Finding the money for Ochirma involved several people (the mother, the cousin and the mother's colleagues) and several acts of support that channelled (public) money, for a limited period of time, into Ochirma's wallet.

Gaining access to money is a serious problem for many people in Aga today, in particular when they are under pressure to pay back instalments within deadlines. In many cases, debt is not handled individually, but through networks of mutual support. If unable to pay back the instalment by their own means, which happens frequently, people try to 'find' money (*naiti den'gi*). This means that relatives or acquaintances are contacted who might be able and willing to lend money. Borrowing money through personal networks has become very difficult over the past few years, either because people have urgent financial troubles themselves or because they are afraid that the borrower will not be able to return the money. Usually, only very close relatives are willing to help out with large sums – provided that they have the money. Support is also necessary in case someone has a 'black credit history' (*chernaia kreditnaia istoriia*), which means that they have not paid their instalments in time. In such a case, it is unlikely that the banks will grant further credit. If they are desperate for money, people sometimes ask others to take out a loan for them. When the unofficial debtor is then unable to pay back the money, such a practice may put a serious strain on social relationships. The following question published in the local newspaper reveals such a problem: 'My relative asked me to take a loan for him from the Sberbank. He paid instalments for a year but then he stopped paying. I cannot get in touch with him, he has been avoiding me for half a year already. I have no documents proving the transfer of money to his account. What can I do in this case?'[7]

Bank employees may find themselves in the difficult position of being caught between social obligation and professional responsibility. A relative might expect them, for example, to give them access to further credit, as in the case reported to me by a Sberbank employee. She knew very well that her uncle would not be able to repay the money to the bank. On the other hand, she felt that she could not deny him the favour. The young woman tried to solve the problem by pretending that she was very busy and asked a colleague to deal with her uncle.

Debt is a collective problem in Aga. Even those who have anticipated the risks of consumer credit and have been careful not to borrow large sums or those with fairly good salaries are concerned because they all have relatives in difficult financial situations who expect their support. The above examples show that money has become deeply implicated in the informal economy of support.

Capitalism and the Logic of Support

Not only has money become part of the economy of support, but the logics of support have also become inscribed in market exchange. This I will demonstrate with reference to the following two cases. My friend Baatar, the entrepreneur mentioned above, operated a small repair service for technological devices in Aginskoe in 2014. Once I chatted to him about the significance of 'good connections' (*khoroshie sviazi*) in the local economy. During the course of our conversation, Baatar told me how a good friend of his came to the service point to refill her printer cartridge. Usually he charges six hundred roubles for the service, but as it was a good friend, he asked her to pay three hundred roubles. Thus, he charged her for the material, but not for the service. There was another customer in the shop who also needed a cartridge refill. Baatar refilled her cartridge and charged the usual price of six hundred roubles. The woman complained that he had taken only three hundred roubles from the previous customer and was now asking her to pay a much higher price. He laughed and asked her whether they were friends. If they became friends, he joked, he would give her a refill for three hundred roubles next time. To charge only half the price for the refill was a form of support Baatar provided to his friend. It is entirely unclear whether this act of support will be reciprocated in the future. But his friend will remember that she has received support and therefore will be inclined to help if possible. If Baatar will need her support at some point, his friend will feel most likely feel obliged to provide it. If, for example, she finds employment in the hospital and he needs treatment, he might be able to jump the queue. In the event that that she is working in a café, he could probably eat there should he be short of money. And if her husband is a bus driver, his children might ride the bus without paying. Given the constant shortage of money that people are experiencing, it is very important to be part of such nonmonetary networks of mutual support. Baatar is happy to support a considerable group of people – he has a large family and many acquaintances in Aga – by providing services to them without making a significant profit. In order to understand how he can conduct commercial business under these circumstances, it is necessary to understand that he participates in a wider economy of support that guarantees him the help of others when he will need it.

The ideal of mutual support has an impact not only on entrepreneurial strategies but also on consumer behaviour. I have repeatedly observed that people buy their clothes not in the shops that offer the lowest prices or that have the greatest choice, but in the shops of their relatives or acquaintances, in order to support their businesses. One January day in 2015, I went with my friend Ganzhima to the market. We wanted to spend some time together rather than to buy anything, and the market was one of the few places warm enough to hang out. Ganzhima led me straight to the little shop of her close friend's mother. She chatted to the elderly woman and asked her about her children and her business. As it turned out, the woman now shared her space in the market with a colleague because the currency crisis was making their business less and less profitable. My friend then looked around the shop and found a few shirts she liked. She asked whether they were offered for sale by her acquaintance. The woman replied that the shirts were being offered for sale by her colleague. Ganzhima put them back, saying that in this case, she would not buy them. This little incident suggests that consumer decisions may depend entirely on the relationship between the salesperson and the customer. It was neither the quality nor the price of the product, nor Ganzhima's consumer needs or desires that led to her decision not to buy the shirts; her decision depended on the question of who would benefit from her purchase. As this case underlines, support is not tied to individuals. Ganzhima did not know the shopkeeper very well, but she knew that she was her good friend's close relative. This was reason enough to decide that she was a person whom she should support.

Supporting someone by buying from them is tied to an expectation: the trader is expected to grant the buyer credit. This causes immense problems for traders who rely on capital to stock up their little shops. Often, their travel to China, where they go in order to buy what they then sell on Russian markets, depends on when they will receive the money owed to them by their customers. One of my informants, Nomidma, has an aunt working as a trader in Aginskoe. She used to help her out in her shop from time to time when the aunt was in China. She also frequently bought clothes from her aunt. The aunt would give her a discount and would also allow a considerable delay in payment. This, as Nomidma told me, had changed recently. The aunt now asked for her money after only three days. From Nomidma's perspective, this violated the rules of mutuality. She said that under these circumstances, she would now buy clothes from her aunt only if she truly liked them and otherwise would buy them elsewhere. This case, along with those of the Sberbank employee who did not want to deal with her uncle and Nomidma's cousin who had to lend money that she received for her electricity bills, exemplifies how the new significance of money and debt accounts for tensions and challenges within intimate social relations. This is also crucial with regard to MLM and pyramid schemes, and will be discussed at length in Chapter 4.

The examples discussed in this section show that the logic of support permeates the commercial sphere. It affects flows of money and at the same time serves the cultivation of relationships and the reassurance of mutual obligation. The logic of the market is not opposed to mutuality, but, on the contrary, requires mutuality in order to deal with the problems and challenges generated by the wider economic system.

Conclusion

In this chapter I have sketched the major developments in Aga's economy following the collapse of the Soviet Union, providing an impression of what capitalism looks like in rural Siberia and how it has been experienced by local people. I have highlighted the new significance of money in the post-Soviet economy and I have shown that this has become a major problem in a remote region where there are few opportunities to make money and where people have become entrapped in relations of debt. Rather than being an exhilarating experience of individual freedom and equal chances for everyone, capitalism presents itself as a constant struggle for money linked to instability, vulnerability and uncertainty – broken only by a minor miracle that disappeared as swiftly as it had appeared. As the following chapter will show, this experience provides a fertile ground for MLM and pyramid schemes.

Capitalism in Russia, just like socialism, has to be understood as being underwritten by a system of informal relations. This is the case at the macrolevel, as exemplified by the deal between Kobzon and Zhamsuev that led to Aga becoming a special economic zone. It is also true at the microlevel, as I have shown in my descriptions of the dense system of mutual support. In Buryat society, I have argued, this is particularly pronounced because the ingrained practice of *blat* merges with a strong moral imperative to support one another economically. Notably, as in the Soviet economy of shortage, informal acts of support are important to ease the shortcomings of the macroeconomic system. Whereas in Soviet times this meant dealing with a shortage of goods, today it means dealing with a shortage of money. The crucial point I made in the second part of this chapter is that in Aga, informal networks, and not merely market mechanisms, determine economic decision making and flows of money to a significant degree. In the following chapters, I explore the intertwining of informal social bonds with capitalist market relations in the operation of MLM and pyramid schemes, both of which frequently cut across the realms of self-interest and of mutuality while growing through intimate social ties.

Notes

1. See website of the Aga district's administration (Administratsiia Aginskogo Buriatskogo Okruga); retrieved 5 November 2018 from http://www.aginskoe.ru/node/35.
2. Names are anonymized throughout the book.
3. The average wage in the district in 2012 was 16,044 roubles (around $241), while the average pension was 7,681 roubles (around $116) (Zabaikalkraistat 2013).
4. A total of 862 people in the district in 2012 (Zabaikalkraistat 2013).
5. Literally translated as 'restructuring', this term refers to Mikhail Gorbachev's policy of reforming the Communist Party during the 1980s.
6. To be found under the entry 'Kredit potrebitel'skii'.
7. Aginskaia Pravda (20 December 2014).

2

American Dream or Pyramid Scheme?

> 'We call our company Amway,' I said in those early 'Selling America' speeches, 'because the American way of private ownership and free enterprise is the best way.' ... Our critics pointed to the socialist economic policies of Chairman Mao, Premier Khrushchev, and Comrade Castro as the wave of the future. Now our critics are no longer laughing. The communist dream is dead.
>
> —Richard DeVos, *Compassionate Capitalism*

In his book, Amway founder Richard DeVos praises his vision of 'good' capitalism. Amway, so the subtitle suggests, provides an opportunity for 'people helping people help themselves'. In the introduction, DeVos writes about his acquaintance from East Germany, a man he calls Andrej Zubail. After one of the speeches the author gave in Berlin, Andrej and his family made their way to the platform:

> 'Mr DeVos', he said softly in heavily accented English, 'I am Andrej Zubail. This is my wife and these are my sons.' For a moment the young man smiled down at his family. Then suddenly he looked up at me. I could tell that he was struggling to find the right words. When he finally spoke, his lips were trembling and a single tear trickled down his cheek. I could see that even as he held his infant sons, his hands were shaking with excitement. 'When freedom came to East Germany,' he said, 'I didn't know what to do first. I wanted everything for Maria and the children, everything we have not these many years. But knowing where to start ... not easy. We had no money – no, is it said, equity? – to get a loan, nothing to sell or trade. We wanted to start a business of our own, but how?' He paused and looked at his wife for moral support. She smiled at him and put her arm around his waist. 'So I say to Maria, "What shall we do?"

> And she answer, "Now we are free. We can do anything."' Andrej went on to thank all of us for the opportunity our company had given him. In just six months, he and Maria had created an impressive small business. But Andrej's story is not about Amway. It is about compassionate capitalism and the remarkable difference it can make in our lives even in small doses. (DeVos 1993: 13–14)

With missionary fervour, MLM companies like Amway promote the American Dream in the sense of the 'devout belief that tomorrow can and will be better than today' (Samuel 2012: 6) around the globe. Claiming to be the messengers and teachers of capitalist modernity, they promise wealth to all who are willing to recruit followers and make the schemes grow. As the quote above shows, DeVos sees Amway as making business accessible even to what he describes as the poor and disoriented *Homo Sovieticus*.

This chapter aims to explore the origins of an unusual industry, an industry characterized by its specific way of selling the products it manufactures. I will show how this industry developed and how it managed to flourish around the world. Moreover, it is important to clarify the structural relationship between MLM and pyramid schemes, elaborating on their similarities and differences. The last part of this chapter deals with the recent history and organization of MLM and pyramid schemes in Aga. Here, I show how MLM and pyramid schemes appeared in Russia and how people in Siberia encounter them.

From Peddling to Direct Selling

As noted by Biggart (1989), the centuries-old business of peddling can be seen as the precursor of direct selling. Until the mid nineteenth century, peddlers in the United States were an important distribution channel for farmers and general stores, as well as a crucial source of supply for the rural population who had limited access to retail shops in towns and cities. Improvement of infrastructure made it possible for manufacturers to supply larger markets, including shops in rural areas. As the number of retail stores increased, many peddlers became shop owners. Peddling did not disappear as a way of distributing products, but it became increasingly organized. While peddlers sold the goods of various producers independently, the new salespeople were recruited by a single manufacturer. Direct selling developed as a retail channel that was seen by some manufacturers to have certain advantages over department stores. In the stores, the products competed with similar products, while direct selling allowed for personal advertisement along with a certain convenience for the customer (Biggart 1989: 20–24).

One of the most successful early direct selling companies was the Fuller Brush Company, which was founded in 1906 and sold brushes. Alfred C. Fuller started his business by making and selling the brushes himself. By 1910, he employed six people producing the brushes and 25 salespeople. His salesmen paid six US dollars for a sample case, brushes and a descriptive list of the products, and were given an exclusive territory for door-to-door selling. They did not receive salaries, but a commission on their sales. Fuller's company expanded quickly and by the mid 1920s, the company had not only developed an elaborate organizational structure, but also had salesmen all over the United States and Canada, who were hired, trained and motivated by a number of branch managers (Friedman 2004: 203–9). As Fuller's autobiography (1960) shows, the idea of the self-made man who lifts himself out of poverty by working hard and by envisaging a better future – a core notion of the American Dream – was anchored in the direct selling industry from its beginning.

Fuller salespeople were given instructions regarding the best strategies for selling. As they were not always welcome, the first challenge was to be let into the house. In order to spark the interest of potential customers, the company offered a small brush as a free sample. The salespeople were advised that in case the housewife wanted the sample but not to see the demonstration, they should say that the brush was on the bottom of their sample case and that they would need to come inside to find it. This gave them time to advertise the brushes. For the demonstration, Fuller salesmen were encouraged to use the body brushes on themselves while explaining their advantages. Their instructions read: 'Rub on hand briskly; *enthuse*' and 'go through motions as if taking a bath' (cited in Friedman 2004: 205). They were also asked to carry an old brush and to look disgusted when speaking about how unhygienic and even dangerous it would be to use such a brush. For Fuller, personal sales were more than simply a channel of distribution; it was a way of advertising his brushes by sparking enthusiasm for the product. Motivating the salesmen, and encouraging them to think positively, was a crucial part of the business, as many were hesitant to knock on doors, afraid of disturbing people in their domestic routines (Friedman 2004: 206).

The growth of the direct selling industry was fuelled by technological innovation in consumer goods. A number of labour-saving devices for households such as washing machines, refrigerators and vacuum cleaners were marketed through direct sales (Friedman 2004: 195–96).

By the 1920s, direct sales were offering serious competition to retail stores, which lobbied against the emerging industry and tried to discredit it by accusing salespeople of dishonesty. In order to counter such accusations and to represent the industry's interests, ninety-one firms formed the 'National Association of Direct Selling Companies' (NADSC) in 1925 (Biggart 1989: 31–32).

Roosevelt's New Deal reforms of the 1930s, which were designed to restore economic health after the Depression, limited the power and freedom of corporations, and had an important impact on the direct selling industry. It now had to comply with the National Industrial Recovery Act, which established trade codes aimed at creating fair business conditions as well as fair labour conditions. The most serious challenge that the economic reforms posed to the industry was the Social Security Act of 1935. The relationship between employer and employee, which had previously been only loosely regulated, was defined more precisely and a minimum wage was introduced. This was a particular problem for direct selling companies because their relationship with their workforce was unusual at the time. Many distributors worked only part time and as the turnover of the sales force was high, there was a constant need for recruitment. Moreover, the workers were dispersed and their selling behaviour could not be controlled. In short, a minimum wage would have ruined the companies. The problem was solved by redefining the salespeople as independent contractors. As such, direct selling companies could avoid the obligation of a minimum wage or unemployment insurance for their salesforce. The salespeople were legally independent, responsible for themselves and, under this framework, continued to provide a cheap supply of labour for the companies (Biggart 1989: 33–41).

Whereas the first salespeople were men, during the mid twentieth century, the industry underwent a process of feminization, which was important to sustaining its success. The feminization of the MLM salesforce was part of a more widespread process of increasing female participation in the labour market. Direct selling appealed to women because its flexibility enabled them to combine their family and household duties. Importantly, unlike other jobs, the direct selling industry was not constrained by gender hierarchies. Anyone could participate and no great investment was required so to do (Biggart 1989: 53–60; Clarke 1999: 78–90). Women played a crucial role in the development of a new sales format during the 1950s: the home party. The party format, popularized by Tupperware vice-president Brownie Wise, gathered an audience in a home during which products were demonstrated. The salesperson would find a hostess willing to invite her friends and neighbours to her house for this purpose. After the demonstration, there would be an opportunity to purchase the products and the hostess received a gift product dependent on the amount of sales made at her party. Home parties combined sociality with the aura of modernity and thrived on the social obligation to reward the hostess for her hospitality (Clarke 1999: 78–86).

From Direct Selling to Multilevel Marketing

Some of the early direct selling companies offered their salespeople a 'finder's fee', which rewarded them for recruiting more salesmen and saleswomen. The purpose of this business strategy was articulated at the NADSC annual convention in 1929:

> We originally put it on the so-called friendship basis. We feel our men are very close to the organization, but they are very busy during the day time and sometimes at night, and it makes it rather difficult to ask them to take a certain amount of their own time without some compensation. However, when we offered a five dollar prize for each man who obtained another who signed up and paid his deposit [on a sales kit], plus a very small percentage of that man's gross sales for the first sixty days, what did we get? We got a new man who paid his deposit, and we received the vital interest of the salesman who obtained that man, to help the new man along the rough spots during his spare times, so that the original salesman would obtain a certain amount of additional recompense by virtue of the gross business done. Of course, there is a minimum that man would have to do before that gross goes into effect, but it is so small that a man has to be a very poor salesman, indeed, in order not to qualify. (Cited in Biggart 1989: 45)

The introduction of multilevel marketing in the 1940s put more emphasis on the idea of the 'finder's fee'. Unlike previous direct selling practice, it was no longer the branch manager who was responsible for recruiting a salesforce; rather, all salespeople were encouraged to engage in recruitment. They could now not only earn a commission on their own sales, but also be rewarded for the sales of their so-called 'downline' – the people they recruited, plus the people recruited by their recruits and so forth. What was now being marketed was not merely a company's product, but also its business opportunity. The salespeople, who were increasingly called 'distributors', 'partners' or 'independent representatives' (I will use the term 'distributor' in this book as this is most common in the MLM literature), now had an interest not only in selling goods but also in recruiting people into their network who would do the same. This innovation created multiple

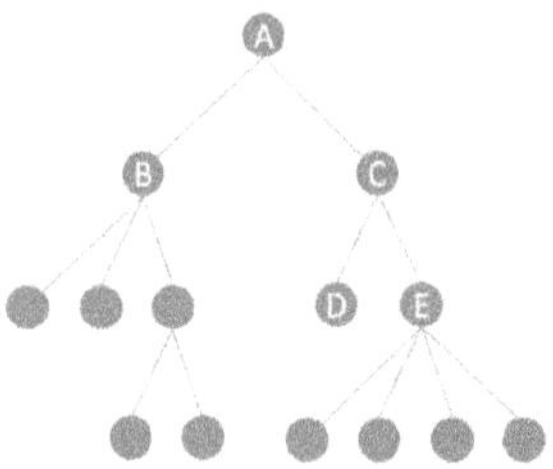

Example of a compensation structure:

Direct commission: 25%

Override commission:

Level 1: 10%

Level 2: 5%

Figure 2.1 MLM reward system.

In MLM, distributors profit from the sales of their downline distributors. Thus, A not only receives a commission on her own sales, but also on the sales of B and C, and on the sales of everyone in their respective downline. A therefore has an interest that her downline works actively and will be ready to also support D and E with training and advice on how to sell and recruit. As we can see in this figure, not all distributors are equally successful in building downlines. D, for example, did not recruit further participants, whereas E managed to attract four participants. People further up in the structure (like A or B and C) rely on the work of those they recruit in order to make their pyramid grow and to increase their profit.

Companies operating according to this model have different compensation structures, but here is an example. The company offers a direct commission of 25 per cent on the sale of products and override commissions of 10 per cent for the first level and 5 per cent for the second level. Let us assume that A sells products worth $1,000, B and C sell products worth $500 and D and E sell products worth $100. All of them would get the 25 per cent on their direct sales. This would be $250 for A, $125 for B and C, and $25 for D and E. In addition, A earns a commission on the sales of all of them. She would get $50 for the sales of B, $50 for the sales of C, $5 for the sales of D and $5 for the sales of E. In total, A would earn $360. C gets an additional commission on the sales of D and E and would earn $145 in total. Compensation schemes often include more than two levels and in addition they offer complicated bonus systems – for example, if a distributor recruits a certain number of people or a distributor's downline reaches a certain sales volume, he or she gets extra rewards. Moreover, there are usually registration fees that have to be paid initially. Distributors are also pressured to buy marketing materials and to attend costly business seminars that are organized by the companies.

levels of salespeople forming a pyramid structure linked through a network of financial relations (Keep and Vander Nat 2014: 192–96). It also enhanced the possibility of making big money in the industry. Distributors learned that if they succeeded in recruiting a large number of people who would sell actively, they could make a fortune. Given this possibility, their efforts shifted from selling to recruiting and, as a result, the industry became somewhat estranged from its products.

One of the first multilevel marketing companies was Nutrilite. Founded in 1934 as the California Vitamin company, it adopted the multilevel model in 1945. While control over the salesforce had been limited in direct selling from the start, it was reduced even further under the MLM model. Direct selling companies would often assign their salespeople a certain territory that was no longer possible in MLM. Distributors were likely to compete on a given territory and the companies no longer had precise information regarding the whereabouts of their salespeople. With the further decentralization of recruitment and training of new salespeople, the companies increasingly lacked control over their distributors' activities and their compliance with the companies' policies. A serious problem was false product claims made by distributors in order to increase their sales. The Food and Drug Administration accused Nutrilite of making 'extravagant therapeutic claims' about the effects of its food additives and vitamins, and also of suggesting to people that they had some deficiency that would need to be cured through the consumption of its products (Keep and Vander Nat 2014: 192–93).

In 1959, two Nutrilite distributors, Jay Van Andel and Richard DeVos, founded their own MLM company, Amway (American Way Association), which played a major role in popularizing the new marketing model and today is the world's largest MLM scheme. Direct selling organizations increasingly adopted the MLM model and by 2009, 90 per cent of American direct selling companies were multilevel firms (Albaum and Peterson 2011: 349). The possibility of making money through chain recruitment that thus became common throughout the direct sales industry led to the industry's resemblance with illegal pyramid schemes, which are based on the very same logic. MLM blurred the boundary between the legal and the illegal, and made the direct selling industry prone to accusations of running pyramid schemes. In 1979, the Federal Trade Commission launched an investigation into Amway to determine whether its network constituted an illegal pyramid. However, the company was not found guilty, largely because it had policies in place that were designed to ensure retail sales. These policies included the rule that 70 per cent of a distributor's monthly purchases had to be resold and that the products had to be sold to at least ten different customers. These policies were regarded by the judge as being sufficient to prove that the emphasis of the schemes was on moving the product through a wholesale and retail network (Keep and Vander Nat 2014: 197). This 1979 case was important because for the first time, a court distinguished an illegal pyramid scheme from a legal MLM scheme. The result of the investigation not only allowed Amway to continue its business, but also helped to legitimize the MLM model (Jones 2011: 11).

The Globalization of Multilevel Marketing

Up until the 1980s, the direct selling industry was proliferating in the United States. In a 1976 national survey of US households commissioned by the Direct Selling Association, almost 16 per cent of the respondents reported that they had worked in the direct sales industry at some point (Biggart 1989: 50). Data provided by the Direct Selling Association shows a continual growth in sales volume and numbers of distributors from the late 1950s until the early 1980s, when development began to stagnate as a result of market saturation (Biggart 1989: 50–51). The direct selling industry had recognized the potential of foreign markets early. Avon opened a branch office in Montreal in 1914 (Keep and Vander Nat 2014: 200–5), Tupperware formally expanded into Europe in the 1960s (Clarke 1999: 185–96) and Amway opened its first overseas office in Sydney, Australia in 1971 (Amway 2018). In Mexico, the first direct selling companies, Avon and Tupperware, began operating in the 1950s (Cahn 2011: 12) and in Thailand direct sales already existed in the 1960s (Wilson 2004: 165). Subsequently, the direct selling industry appears to have boomed in countries such as Thailand, Mexico and China in the late 1980s and early 1990s, in the context of neoliberal economic reforms (Cahn 2011; Jeffery 2001; Wilson 2004). Furthermore, technological and infrastructural progress sparked intensified economic globalization, which facilitated the spread of direct selling in the Global South and, after the fall of the Iron Curtain, into the formerly socialist world (Wilson 1999). The ability to expand into new markets fuelled the industry. In fact, given the saturation of U.S. markets, it could be assumed that it saved the industry from decline, in particular as legal restrictions on direct selling became stronger in the United States. By the 1990s, 49 per cent of Avon's pre-tax profit relied on sales made in developing countries, 80 per cent of Tupperware's revenue came from countries outside the

United States and Amway's foreign branches accounted for 70 per cent of its $6.8 billion in annual sales (Cahn 2011: 51–53). Today, the direct selling industry makes more than 50 per cent of its sales outside Europe and the United States. Whilst in terms of sales volume, the United States, China, Japan, Korea and Germany are the top five global markets, in terms of numbers of distributors, Russia ranks seventh, behind the United States, Indonesia, Thailand, Korea, China and India, with over five million distributors in 2017 (World Federation of Direct Selling Associations 2018a).

The World Federation of Direct Selling Associations (WFDSA) states on its website that direct sellers include 'individuals who are career minded entrepreneurs building their own businesses or part-time entrepreneurs earning extra income. Most enjoy significant discounts on products. In fact, some choose only to enjoy and use the products and not to sell at all'. The lobby organization puts in euphemistic terms what is perceived by its critics as the selling of empty dreams. The industry not only faces legal problems in the United States, but also in other parts of the world. In Britain, for example, Amway was accused in 2007 of breaking company law by making false promises. According to an investigation initiated by the government, only 10 per cent of the company's distributors in Britain make any profit. Amway's main activity, it was suggested, was encouraging people to join the salesforce, enabling the company to earn registration fees and to sell marketing materials (Brown 2007). Amway's barristers convinced the court that the company would make substantial changes to its business model in the United Kingdom, including suspending the sale of marketing materials and terminating contracts with distributors who made exaggerated claims. The Secretary of State for the Department of Business, Enterprise and Regulatory Reform (BERR) appealed against the decision, arguing that if the court had found the old business model unacceptable, Amway should be shut down. In 2009, however, the court's decision was confirmed, the judgment declaring that the company had failed to control its distributors, but had not engaged in deliberate dishonesty (Jones 2011: 165–66).

The difficulty in evaluating what opportunities MLM really offers results from the lack of data collected by investigators who are independent of the industry (Keep and Vander Nat 2014: 203–4). Flows of products and services through direct distribution channels are extremely hard, if not impossible, to track. The industry itself reports growth, which, given the above-cited figures, can at least partly be attributed to international expansion (cf. Keep and Vander Nat 2014). A major problem with the information value of sales figures is that the industry appears to be selling mainly to its own distributors rather than to external customers. As I will show later in this study, internal consumption is indeed crucial to the industry's ability to generate profits and high pressure is exerted on distributors by their uplines to consume their company's products to excess. It is important to distinguish between external and internal consumption because 'arguments that treat internal and external consumption the same blur the nature of the selling opportunity and ignore the potential for ongoing recruitment to be the primary source for compensating participants – a key characteristic of a pyramid scheme' (Keep and Vander Nat 2014: 204). Thus, as I will discuss in the following section in more detail, the involvement of products or services cannot be taken as a defining characteristic that neatly separates MLM from pyramid schemes.

The globalization of the MLM industry was manifested not only in the expansion of companies with headquarters in the United States, but also in the worldwide proliferation of the business model. Many new direct selling companies were founded in various parts of the world, including Mistine in Thailand (Wilson 2004), Omnilife in Mexico (Cahn 2011) and NL International in Russia, and these companies also proliferated across borders. In Siberia, I discovered direct selling companies founded in China, Germany, Russia, Sweden and the United States. As the business model globalized, MLM began operating in economic environments very different from that of the United States. As in the United States, national legislation played an important role in the ways in which the industry developed. In China, for example, MLM was prohibited in 1998. According to Jeffery's (2001) analysis, the Chinese government banned MLM because it challenged the authority of the Communist Party. However, the ban did not mean that the industry disappeared. Amway, for example, restructured its sales system in China so that it could continue to operate, and today China is Amway's largest foreign market (Jones 2011: 145–52).

The origins of the MLM industry in the cultural context of the United States have played an important role in its globalization, particularly in developing countries. The appeal of the marketing model is enhanced by the notions of capitalist modernity that are attached to it precisely because of its American roots. Jeffery (2001: 67–70) observed that in Chinese MLM circles, myths regarding the popularity and acceptance of MLM in the United States were widespread. Moreover, a sense of participating in the global market was of central importance for MLM distributors in China. I made similar observations in Russia, upon which I will elaborate in the next chapter. It is particularly noteworthy that in countries such as Russia and China, where the United States are generally viewed very critically in media and political discourse, an economic model that is strongly associated with the United States is embraced by a significant number of people.

An Industry on the Brink of Legitimacy

There are various types of pyramid schemes. What they have in common is that consumers or investors are promised large profits that are based on their recruitment of others rather than on real investments or sales. Pyramid schemes rely on the continual recruitment of further investors in order to compensate participants, because early investors are paid with the money of subsequent investors. Often, pyramid schemes purport to be lucrative business projects in order to mask their pyramid structure. Products and services may be involved, but they play only a marginal role in the schemes. The rules regarding recruitment and the recoupment of money vary across pyramid schemes. However, in all schemes, financial gain depends on one's position in the pyramid and on the growth of the scheme. Essentially, we are dealing with money transfer schemes that benefit a small number of people at the top of the pyramid, while resulting in a loss of money for the majority of investors. Pyramid schemes can survive for several years, but they are doomed to collapse when their growth stagnates.

As indicated above, the introduction of further levels into direct selling made MLM very similar to pyramid schemes and also it allowed pyramid schemes to hide behind the MLM industry. Consequently, the growth of the MLM industry facilitated the proliferation of fraudulent pyramid schemes. Given their similarity, there are many cases in which it is unclear whether a venture can be classified as MLM or as a pyramid scheme. As described above, Amway faced the accusation of being a pyramid scheme, as did many other direct selling companies using the MLM model (Keep and Vander Nat 2014). Only recently, Michael Johnson, Herbalife's CEO and America's best-paid chief executive, was vehemently accused by hedge fund manager Bill Ackman of running a modern-day 'Ponzi scheme'. Ackman lamented that Herbalife was duping the company's salespeople by promising them that they could become millionaires (Neate 2012). Herbalife rejected the allegations, but the Federal Trade Commission (FTC) investigated the company for seventeen months. The FTC's policy in pursuing cases of alleged MLM fraud is highly opaque and the legislation with regard to pyramid schemes is fuzzy. Asked by *New York Times* reporter Joe Nocera last year

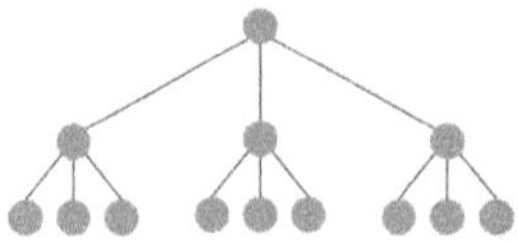

Example of a compensation structure:

Initial investment: $500

Level 1 commission: $150

Level 2–4 commission: $30

Like MLM, pyramid schemes have various compensation schemes. Unlike most MLM ventures, there are usually very high 'registration fees' or initial investments. Here is an example that was provided by the U.S. Federal Trade Commission (1998) as a typical case for a pyramid scheme. In this scheme, each investor has to pay an initial sum of $500. Investors are instructed to build downlines by recruiting three further participants who should each also recruit three participants and so on. The investor is promised $150 for each new investor he or she recruits and a $30 commission for each recruit at the next three levels. In total, the investor is promised commissions for four levels of participants below him or her. To the potential investor, this may look like a great opportunity. It seems that they can earn $3,960 on an investment of $500: $150 from the first level of three recruits is $450; $30 from the next three levels of recruits is $270 ($30 x 9), plus $810 ($30 x 27), plus $2,430 ($30 x 81). We should also consider the scheme from its promoter's perspective: the promoter receives $500 from each investor and at the most he or she has to pay $240 in commissions to earlier investors in the new recruit's upline. The promoter has to pay $150 to the person who recruited the new member and $30 to each of the three longer-standing participants in the new member's upline. Thus, the promoter will keep more than half of the $500 that was paid by the new member. Mathematics shows that most investors will find themselves at the bottom of the scheme when it collapses. Given their structure at the time of their collapse, 70 per cent of investors will not have recouped their investment and will have lost their initial $500 payment.

In the cases I observed in Siberia, the compensation plans of the schemes were more complicated than this and highly opaque. They included rules about how many people one must recruit to earn anything at all, rules regarding the timespan within which one has to achieve this, and promises of various kinds of bonus payments. As in MLM, pyramid scheme participants may be encouraged to buy marketing materials and to attend business training sessions.

Figure 2.2 Pyramid scheme reward system.

what distinguished an illegal pyramid scheme from a legal multilevel marketing company, an FTC spokesman said: 'Lots of reporters have asked that question. Our final response is, We're not going to answer it' (quoted in Nocera 2015). In the 1979 FTC investigation of Amway, the company was able to convince the Commission of its good business practice with the argument that it was selling its products to 'real' customers and not simply to other recruits. As Nocera points out, many MLM companies used the same argumentation to counter allegations that they were running pyramid schemes, using the Amway case as a precedent. Although not codified in law, the FTC seemed to accept this argument as a way of distinguishing MLM from pyramid schemes. However, in a recent law case involving a pyramid scheme called BurnLounge, the court ruled that it did not matter whether the customer was inside or outside the network; rather, the court decided that the test was 'whether a company's "primary" purpose involved recruiting rather than "meaningful opportunities for retail sales"' (Nocera 2015). In practice, this distinction can be extremely difficult to assess. It is not surprising, therefore, that people who join schemes are not always sure whether they are dealing with MLM or with a pyramid scheme.

The rise of the MLM industry facilitated the existence of pyramid scams and, if seen from a critical perspective, it could be suggested that MLM *is* a form of pyramid scam. Yet, in terms of their history, it is important to pay attention to details. Investment fraud existed long before MLM and the idea underlying it can be traced back to the early days of capitalism. As Bakan (2005) describes in his history of the corporation, in the late seventeenth and early eighteenth centuries, stockbrokers in London were looking for investors to whom they could sell shares in bogus companies that quickly collapsed. Essentially, this is what Charles Ponzi, an Italian immigrant to the United States, did in 1919. Ponzi initiated a fraudulent scheme by offering massive returns on investments in a business involving the buying and selling of international postal coupons. In fact, the business Ponzi claimed to be highly profitable was not feasible on a large scale. Eventually, the fraud was detected, the scheme collapsed and Ponzi was arrested (*New York Times*, 13 August 1920). What distinguished Ponzi's scheme from the bogus companies advertised by early London stockbrokers was its sheer scale (he managed to attract over 40,000 investors) and the fact that he started returning money to early investors, thus cultivating the illusion that his business was indeed profitable. Unlike the pyramid schemes that resemble MLM, Ponzi's scheme only had a single level. Investors were not rewarded for recruiting further 'shareholders'.

Thus, if we compare direct selling in its early days to Ponzi's scheme, it is clearly very different. Their similarity begins only with the introduction of the multiple-level or pyramid structure accompanied by complex systems of compensation.

Hardly any research has been done on pyramid schemes and little is known about their history. In at least some cases, pyramid schemes develop out of failed business ventures that are then turned into pyramid schemes in order to attract investments. To my knowledge, there are no studies that have looked at the initial intentions of those who set up pyramid schemes. Furthermore, it might be the case that MLM inspired fraudsters to combine Ponzi's idea with that of a reward-for-recruitment system, but I have not found any sources that either confirm or refute this idea. Moreover, it is unclear whether the globalization of MLM was and is related to the dissemination of pyramid schemes. However, there is some evidence that in places where MLM proliferates, pyramid schemes are flourishing. As shown above, pyramid schemes have been an issue in the United States for several decades. In China, the second-largest market for MLM after the United States, pyramid schemes are also a massive problem. As the Xinhua News Agency reported, in the first eleven months of 2008, almost 4,000 pyramid schemes were closed down by the government in the country (Lim 2009). People invest their live savings and sell their houses in order to put money into schemes that pretend to be direct selling enterprises built on Western business models. According to research carried out by the *Financial Times*, every Chinese province recorded at least one pyramid scheme collapse between 2014 and 2015. The money being paid into schemes that collapsed in 2014 amounted to more than $16 billion. One of the schemes investigated by the *Financial Times* involved 135,000 farmers in Hebei province who each paid more than an average annual household income into a 'rural cooperative', the collapse of which devastated whole families. Several people fled from the region to avoid their creditors (Hornby 2015). As I will briefly discuss below and will show throughout this book, MLM and pyramid schemes in Aga are closely entangled. In several cases, local pyramid scheme operators have been trained in MLM companies, and narratives and ideas emanating from MLM have become part of the stock in trade of pyramid schemes.

Pyramid schemes are a massive problem in many parts of the world. While pyramid schemes are a long-established type of fraud, it appears that their dissemination has been aided by modern technologies (cf. Valentine 1998). Although illegal in most jurisdictions, the difficulty of distinguishing MLM, which is generally accepted as a legal business venture, from illegal pyramid schemes is widespread and many countries have found distinguishing between them in official legislation problematic.

Multilevel Marketing and Pyramid Schemes in Aga

After the fall of the Iron Curtain, formerly socialist territories became an important new market for direct sales. In the face of the economic crisis of the 1990s and rising levels of unemployment, many people were receptive to the business opportunity that MLM seemed to offer. Avon started operating in Russia in 1993, and by 1995 had over 16,000 sales representatives, whilst Mary Kay had 25,000 (Stanley 1996). In 1995 Herbalife opened its first branches in Russia and Tupperware followed in 1997 (Herbalife 2018; Tupperware 2018). Postsocialist countries offered not only new markets for MLM, but also fertile ground for all sorts of pyramid and Ponzi schemes. During the 1990s, a wealth of schemes flourished in Serbia, Bulgaria, Russia, Romania and Albania (Andrews 1997). Some of these pyramids were of huge scale, for example, the Caritas scheme that was launched in Romania in 1992. Caritas touched at least every fifth household in Romania and involved sums that came close to the country's GDP (Verdery 1996: 174). The Russian MMM scheme, which is described in more detail below, was the most spectacular on postsocialist territory, attracting 15 million investors in the course of only six months (Smirnova 2012). In some countries, such as Albania, the schemes had a serious impact on economic development. The Albanian schemes of the 1990s reached such a scale that their collapse caused the national economy to go into recession (Musaraj 2011: 85–86).

The first MLM schemes appeared in Aga in the late 1990s. Among the companies that recruited salespeople in Aga were large international firms like Mary Kay and Avon, but also smaller MLM companies based in Russia and China. People became familiar with the marketing model through these companies. However, the efforts of all these companies were exceeded by Amway, which managed to attract large numbers of distributors, making it the most significant actor in the popularization of the MLM model. Amway expanded into Russia in 2005 and the first Amway entrepreneurs became active in the district about two years later. By 2010, the scheme had gained considerable popularity and, according to the accounts of my informants, registrations peaked locally two years later in 2012. The most successful distributors in Aga, according to their own estimates, had built downlines of more than one thousand people. There is no data regarding the number of distributors in the district, but as several parallel structures exist, it can be assumed that the number of people who signed up to Amway's scheme is well in excess of one thousand.

During the period in which Amway was expanding in Aga, two other major schemes flourished in the region, both of which reached a significant scale, resulting in all my informants being aware of them. One of them was the infamous MMM, a Ponzi scheme that spread across the entire Russian Federation. The scheme was first launched in 1994 by the mathematician Sergei Mavrodi and developed into one of the largest financial scams on formerly socialist territory. Massive advertisement in public space and on television promised 50 per cent interest on investments. After six months, 15 million people had paid their money into the pyramid. Those who came first made a profit, but masses of people lost their money. Several investors committed suicide as a result. Mavrodi was arrested, but, interestingly, people's anger was directed not at him, but at the state, which was said to have spoiled the scheme. The mathematician was elected into Parliament and released from prison. A year later, he lost his status as a deputy, but managed to hide until 2003, when he was once again arrested and imprisoned for four years (Borenstein 1999; Smirnova 2012). In 2011, Mavrodi relaunched MMM, openly declaring on the webpage that it was a 'pyramid' (*piramida*). Casting himself as a philanthropist, he claimed to offer people a system of mutual help. Although people remembered the collapse of the scheme eighteen years before, once again it attracted masses of investors, among them a considerable number of people from Aga.[1] The scheme collapsed in 2012. Enormous sums were lost, leaving people desperate in the face of debt. Many had taken bank loans to put money into MMM and were unable to repay them. Some victims blamed themselves, while others blamed the local operators, some of whom suffered psychological breakdowns as a result of the social pressure put on them to return the money. Those who had withdrawn their money in time and actually made a profit kept this to themselves.

The MMM hype was followed by a significant rush on a pyramid scheme called Light Business Marketing (LBM). LBM and most of the other pyramid schemes I encountered in Aga during my research were different from MMM in three ways: first, unlike MMM, they were not openly declared as 'pyramids'; second, they included a multilevel compensation structure; and, third, they pretended to market products or services. Whereas MMM resembled a large-scale gambling game, LBM and other pyramid schemes appeared as companies (*kompanii*) and functioned like the schemes discussed above, ie, Ponzi's idea combined with a multiple-level bonus system. LBM asked for a registration fee of 5,500 roubles (around $83) and promised people that they could earn money by recruiting further participants and additional money by working online. The work consisted in filling in online forms relating to popular brands. The forms had to be purchased for 650 roubles (around $10) each. How the filling in of online forms generated money was unclear to me and probably to most of the participants, but the virtual money it created could be invested into shares of a hotel complex in Sochi and the returns from these investments were said to make people rich. Across Russia, the scheme attracted more than half a million investors (Savel'ev 2013). In Aga, it operated for around a year before collapsing in 2013. Both MMM and LBM had reached such dimensions that their collapse provoked an investigation by the local authorities. The local promoters of the schemes were found impoverished and therefore could not be charged with financial crime. There were rumours that some people had made money and used it to buy apartments in Ulan-Ude and Moscow. However, the vast majority had lost their money and had no chance of recovering it.

At the time of my research, in 2014 and 2015, several smaller-scale pyramid schemes were being operated in Aga and a number of MLM companies were seeking to sell products and recruit participants. They were pushed by people who called themselves *seteviki*, who firmly believed that the schemes offer a great opportunity for the whole community. The *seteviki* are far from being the only people who register as MLM distributors or pyramid scheme investors, but it is they who constantly strive to recruit new people into their schemes. The vast majority of those who signed up for MLM are people who have realized that the business does not work for them, people who were pressured to participate but had no intention to actively pursue business, and people who registered in order to get a discount on the purchase of products. In the case of pyramid schemes, most people who have invested money simply wait for the promised returns or have already given up the hope that they will see their money again. These nonactive participants often managed to recruit a few people in an initial surge of enthusiasm, but they then quickly realized how difficult and problematic it was to sign up a large number of people and gave up their attempts to do so. They are looked down upon by the active operators of MLM and pyramid schemes, who call them lazy, bemoan their lack of belief in the schemes and criticize their lack of confidence in themselves.

Aga's *seteviki* are predominantly, although not exclusively, female Buryat pensioners. They are often involved in several schemes at the same time, sometimes a combination of MLM and pyramid schemes, or they are pushing only one scheme, but have participated in others in the past. These women are generally aged between fifty-five and sixty-five (retirement age for women in Russia was fifty-five at the time of my research), mostly healthy and willing to work. They belong to a generation that consciously experienced the radical economic, political and social upheavals that followed the collapse of the Soviet Union, and who struggled to raise their children during the severe economic crisis of the 1990s. Some of these women are radical in their pursuit of money, while others are more reluctant. The former try with missionary fanaticism to explain the benefit of the schemes to people, desperately seeking to overcome resistance to participation, while at the other end of the spectrum, involvement is seen more as a potentially profitable hobby. These apparently less committed *seteviki* like to come to the offices to chat to their colleagues and to discuss products or marketing plans. They believe in the companies, but they accept the fact that not everybody is interested in joining the schemes. The social position of these women within family and kinship networks plays an important role in the proliferation of MLM and pyramid schemes, an issue that will be discussed in more detail in Chapter 4.

Seteviki encourage their relatives and friends to buy products, to register as distributors or to pay money into pyramid schemes. Even if they manage to spark only short-lived enthusiasm, in many cases, this has been enough to account for a considerable growth of the schemes. In Aga, the *seteviki*'s knowledge about the schemes is limited and often based on what they are told by the company founders or people higher up in the corporate hierarchy. They want to earn money to supplement their very small pension in order to support their children and grandchildren, and they understand MLM and / or pyramid schemes as offering them full-time or part-time employment.

The MLM product range is usually more interesting for women and thus it is no surprise that the industry is heavily gendered worldwide. However, there are MLM companies that specifically target men by marketing 'male' products, such as car accessories. Amway, in particular, welcomes men and emphasizes that it is a family business rather than a female business. While the active distributors are a fairly homogeneous group, they target the whole breadth of society as potential consumers and recruits. The same is true for pyramid schemes. Whereas the activists in Aga are mostly elderly women, investors include people of all age groups and social standing, male and female, Russian and Buryat. I heard of local politicians who came at night to the MMM operators' houses, wrapped up in their coats, hats pulled down over their faces, to register without being seen by the neighbours. I met a villager who told me that her husband was an alcoholic and her son was in prison, and who, obviously desperate for money, wanted to recruit me into a pyramid scheme. I met an old man, an active participant in the district's public life and author of a dissertation about the Aga Buryats, who joined one scheme after another, and also I met schoolchildren who were sent or taken to the seminars by their parents and were encouraged to invite their classmates into the schemes.

Aga's *seteviki* usually operate MLM or pyramid schemes from small offices located in the towns of the district. They rent the offices on their own initiative and the office rent is usually shared among them. The offices are used for everyday business, such as making phone calls with the purpose of inviting people into the schemes, for studying compensation schemes, product descriptions or the biographies of charismatic representatives, and for dealing with paperwork, such as placing orders or organizing travel to business seminars. The offices are important local centres of the schemes and meeting points for the *seteviki*. Products are usually posted from the sites of production to these offices, where they can be picked up by the *seteviki* and distributed to those who ordered them.

The vast majority of those who work for MLM companies, whether at the time of my fieldwork or previously, earn hardly any money for their work and some have even lost money. They had spent it on registration fees, marketing materials, entrance fees for business seminars, travel to business seminars, products they consumed themselves or products that they found themselves unable to sell. But even when they found people willing to buy the products, the distributors faced a major problem: customers in Aga expect to be granted credit. Thus, payment is often delayed and distributors have no capital with which to replenish stock; even more unfortunately, sometimes payment is never made. While their customers usually pay the distributors in cash, the latter all have bank accounts through which they pay the companies for the products and through which they receive commissions and bonus payments. However, the distributors or former distributors did not necessarily see their involvement as a waste of money. Most had the impression that they had received something for their money, be it business training or products, and tended to blame failure on themselves.

Both MLM and pyramid scheme *seteviki* usually avoided speaking about the actual money they earned and instead preferred emphasizing how much money *could* be earned. Whereas participation in MLM rarely ruins people financially, pyramid schemes have devastating consequences for most investors. This included many of the women who were most actively involved. Along with many other investors, they took expensive consumer loans in order to pay money into the schemes. When the schemes collapsed or payments did not arrive as imagined, they were left with debts that they were often unable to repay.

Everyone I spoke to during my research was aware that fraudulent schemes were being operated in the district. Despite negative experiences, including the embarrassment of having invested in the schemes, social conflict resulting from their collapse and irritation about constant invitations, there seemed to be a general feeling of insecurity and ambiguity associated with the schemes. On the one hand, people demonized them, but on the other hand, many of my informants had not yet given up on the idea that some pyramid schemes might offer a real opportunity. Perhaps, some people thought, it was a matter of timing. If they managed to place themselves at the apex of a new scheme, then they could also profit from it. Others thought that there might not only be fraudulent but also good companies that everyone could profit from. When I told people about my research interest, I was often asked which of the schemes would be the best one, where it was possible to earn money or whether it would be possible to earn money in such schemes at all. Interestingly, both MLM and pyramid schemes were not discussed in terms of morality, but almost exclusively in terms of opportunity. People were concerned by their own inability to correctly assess the opportunities the schemes offered rather than with the question of whether earning money in this way was legitimate.

There is a broad spectrum of opinion in relation to MLM and pyramid schemes in Aga, often stated clearly with respect to certain companies, but ambiguous with regard to the phenomenon as a whole. People say that they like the products of one company but not of another; they think one company to be fraudulent and another company to be promising; they differentiate between MLM and pyramid schemes, and yet they are not sure how to categorize certain companies. I met several people who made clearly negative comments about MLM, but a few months later, they signed up for a scheme. I also frequently encountered people who had lost money in one or several schemes, but nevertheless then invested money again.

Others described how they had suffered not only financially but also psychologically from the collapse of schemes and then went on to tell me about their new 'business projects'. Criticism is private, quiet and often mixed with uncertainty. The local media does not mention the schemes and local politics ignores them as long as they do not reach the dimensions achieved by MMM and LBM. Ulan-Ude newspapers, which are also sold in Aga, are as ambiguous about the schemes as public opinion in general and I found issues that contained warnings about dubious companies along with advertisements for pyramid schemes.

Conclusion

Direct selling was introduced as an innovative form of marketing that from its inception generated particular problems. Working with a dispersed salesforce, companies had only limited control over the selling strategies of their salesforce, while the latter depended on successful sales in order to earn a salary. This made the industry prone to accusations of aggressive selling behaviour and exaggerated claims regarding the quality of the products. The introduction of a multiple-level compensation structure generated further problematic issues. While previously the income of the salespeople had been clearly tied to their sales, the recruitment of further distributors now promised much higher rewards, rendering the entire structure more complex and opaque. Rags-to-riches stories became a more significant element in the marketing of an industry that was now selling opportunities as much as products. However, the hopes that are raised distort the real probability of successful selling and recruitment. In most cases, the distributors' labour is not rewarded because markets are saturated and consumer interest in the products is limited. The companies nevertheless profit from every attempt made, mainly through internal consumption, the occasional sales of a huge salesforce, and the sales of marketing material and business events to participants.

MLM and pyramid schemes occupy a grey area between legitimate economic activity and financial fraud. The fact that both depend upon multiple compensation levels accounts for a structural resemblance between MLM and pyramid schemes, and in some cases it is hard to make a clear distinction between the two. The boundaries between MLM and pyramid schemes are further blurred when we examine their local manifestations. In Aga, both are represented by local people of similar backgrounds, they are operated in the same manner and they make the same promises. In subsequent chapters I will show that the similarities go even deeper and include recruitment strategies, advertising methods and corporate culture.

Note

1. Again, there is no data regarding the exact number of people involved.

3

Spiritual Capitalism

> Tania (Oriflame distributor): It is not without reason that sometimes network marketing is called a sect. Because if someone achieved something they all [cry]: 'Let's applaud', like idiots, 'what a genius', I find it funny myself, just emotions, you know…
>
> Marina: Positive thinking.
>
> Tania: That's why people who are not involved are saying 'this really must be a sect, they are having fun, they are feeling good'.

The resemblance between MLM or pyramid schemes and sects (*sekty*) is frequently noted by outside observers and I witnessed many times how the comparison was also picked up by those actively involved in the schemes, as the above quote exemplifies. Academics have called MLM 'lipstick evangelism' (Dolan and Scott 2009) and have described MLM companies as 'quasi-religious corporations' (Bromley 1995). The comparison suggests itself readily even when one first encounters the people who are involved in the schemes and one becomes a target of their fanatical attempts at recruitment. Although the parallels between religious movements and MLM have been noted, their relationship has not been specified analytically, and pyramid schemes have not been explored ethnographically from this point of view. This chapter seeks to fill this gap by drawing on the examples of two schemes and some of their key representatives in Aga.

The resemblance between MLM and religious movements is not coincidental. Cahn (2006, 2011) has made an important contribution by showing the impact of Christianity upon the formation of the MLM industry. Alfred C. Fuller, who in 1906 founded the Fuller Brush

Company, one of the first direct selling companies, was a devotee of Christian Science. Influenced by the teachings of Mary Baker Eddy, the Christian Science founder and adherent of the New Thought movement, Fuller aligned the spiritual principles in which he believed with his selling business. In his biography, he writes: 'Everyone knows that I ascribe to Christian Science, for I have tried to use Scientific Principle in conducting the business, of which everyone is aware' (Fuller 1960: 129–30). In his ethnography, Cahn demonstrates convincingly how a key teaching of New Thought and also of Christian Faith – the idea that physical reality can be shaped through the power of the mind – has permeated the direct selling industry.

Cahn also points to the corporate genealogy of direct selling companies, which suggests that Fuller's ideas have been directly transferred to other companies. In 1937, Frank Stanley Beveridge, the Fuller vice-president, founded his own company, Stanley Home Products, which quickly became very successful. One of its most successful distributors was Mary Kay Ash, who later started her own company, the now well-known Mary Kay Cosmetics (Cahn 2006: 127–29). As Clarke (1999) shows, both Fuller's and Stanley's sales strategies, along with their quasi-religious corporate philosophies and positive-thinking rhetoric, also had a major impact on the development of Tupperware, which was invented in 1942 by Earl Silas Tupper. The corporate culture of Stanley Home Products as well as Tupperware included sentimental rituals and pilgrimages of enthusiastic distributors to the companies' headquarters (Clarke 1999: 90–91, 139).

The impact of Christianity on the formation of the direct selling industry is further exemplified by Amway, whose founding families are devout believers. Being asked in an interview whether he sees a contradiction between being a successful entrepreneur and a Christian believer, Amway founder Richard DeVos stated the following:

> Being a capitalist is actually fulfilling the will of God in my life. Prayerfully, I trust that this is my calling. So I don't see any contradiction. The alternative view is that, as a believer, I should be poor, a business failure. I do not accept that. God has given us talents. Either we use them in business or we all should become priests and ministers, or devote ourselves to social work. That is not a framework to provide meaningful employment or opportunities for everyone. (DeVos 2010)

To investigate the relationship between the spiritual or religious in MLM and pyramid schemes is important because it allows us to understand their appeal beyond money. Before going into my ethnography in order to demonstrate parallels between religious movements and the schemes, a discussion on the new significance of religion and spirituality after socialism is useful.

Religion and Spirituality after Socialism

After about seven decades of state-imposed secularism, religion gained new popularity and public visibility following the collapse of the Soviet Union. It was not only the 'traditional' religions like Orthodox Christianity, Islam or Buddhism that resurfaced. What took place, Pelkmans (2009) emphasizes, was not merely a revival of religion that had been repressed during socialism. People did not just seek refuge in the tradition and ritual of the established churches; many turned to new charismatic movements such as Pentecostal Christianity, which offer hope in new forms of meaning.

Interestingly, not only was the religious gaining force and attracted adherents in post-Soviet Russia; as Galina Lindquist (2006) shows, magic practices were thriving as well. Lindquist observed an upsurge of paranormal performances and services in the 1990s carried out by magicians, sorcerers and fortune-tellers. There were a number of newspapers the content of which could be described in terms of a New Age discourse, featuring articles about astrology, occult phenomena and advice on how to find inner harmony, beauty and material wealth. Alternative healing practices also became popular and diverse specialists offered to heal diseases through massage, bone-setting, herb medicine or the laying-on the hands (Lindquist 2006: 1–25).

Pelkmans (2009) understands the appeal of charismatic Christianity in formerly socialist countries as being linked to the disturbances, chaos and problems caused by the fall of the Soviet state and the confrontation with the free market. Not only did the institutional structures and the welfare system break down during this period, but a whole ideology also dissolved. Under conditions of uncertainty, disorientation and a struggle for survival, the vision of the future and the community offered by religious movements proved attractive. Similarly, Lindquist (2006) sees economic upheaval as the cause for the proliferation of magic practices and New Age discourse. When other societal channels of agency are blocked, she argues, people seek out alternative ones, such as magic. And when society loses its vision of the future, as was the case with the collapse of the Soviet project, it turns to alternative forms of hope (Lindquist 2006: 9).

Both Pelkmans' and Lindquist's arguments resonate with a key point made by Comaroff and Comaroff (2001), who attribute religious resurgence and the widespread appearance of 'occult economies' visible in phenomena ranging from witchcraft scandals to the resurgence of zombies and money magic, to the 'culture of neoliberalism'. Capitalism at the millennium, they argue, is characterized by the new significance of consumption, whereas production has become somewhat invisible. The value of labour has been displaced by the magic of capital. This is an unsettling experience for people at the margins of the global economy as much as in developed countries, but is particularly so in societies that have recently been subject to significant economic change. Disrupted lives and increasing inequalities have led to feelings of being left out of global prosperity. The Comaroffs contend that occult attempts at money making and the rise of Pentecostal Christianity are responses to the experience of an enigmatic capitalism and express an attempt to come to terms with the puzzlement resulting from new forms of wealth and its techniques: 'of its sources and the capriciousness of its distribution, of the mysterious forms it takes, of its slipperiness, of the opaque relations between means and ends embodied in it' (Comaroff and Comaroff 2001: 7). They are manifestations of a 'messianic, salvific, even magical' capitalism that is linked to the idea of empowering the disempowered.

Although the notion of occult economies is useful within this broader picture and the popularity of MLM and pyramid scheme may well be seen as reactions to uncertain conditions caused by economic and social upheaval, I think it is important to differentiate between various ways through which the spiritual and the economic become entangled. Get-rich-quick schemes are seen by the Comaroffs (2001) as examples of a retreat from the disruptions caused by neoliberal capitalism and as a resort to the magical. They constitute somewhat mystic economies that are thought to generate money from nothing and 'defy explanation in the conventional terms of practical reason' (Comaroff and Comaroff 2001: 19). The Comaroffs describe occult economies as if they occur parallel to another, more formal economy. Although intertwined with it, the spiritual appears as a response to capitalism. Despite discussing a particular spirituality, one preoccupied with the hope of making money and achieving wealth, their account resonates with classical anthropological studies that have observed appearances of spirits in contexts where people have recently become involved in capitalist relations of production (Ong 1987; Taussig 1980).

MLM and pyramid schemes, I want to argue, are different. MLM's positive-thinking spirituality lies at the origins of its historical development. Therefore, it is an interesting example of how capitalism is formed through religious dispositions and attitudes (cf. Weber 2002). Although the enthusiasm with which they have been embraced may well be seen as related to economic change, they are not merely a mystic, occult or religious reaction to capitalism; instead, as I have detailed in the introduction, they are very much *part of* capitalism. We are dealing with an entirely secular global business that is marketed by multinational companies and that, albeit radical, is based on ideas that form the basis of contemporary capitalist thinking.

Daromir Rudnyckyj's (2009) concept of 'spiritual economies' is helpful to clarify my point. Rudnyckyj develops the notion of 'spiritual economies' with the objective of explaining a dimension of the relationship between spirituality and global capitalism that diverges from the Comaroffs' notion of occult economies. The latter captures practices that can be seen as a resort to the supernatural in the face of neoliberal disruptions or as a form of resistance against neoliberal transformations. Rudnyckyj's notion of 'spiritual economies', in contrast, allows us to see spirituality as a component of corporate management aimed at motivating and guiding the workforce. The idea emerges from his research in an Indonesian steel factory in which a spiritual reform was implemented to cultivate the employees' Islamic virtue. The reform obliged the workers to attend spiritual training sessions and it was hoped that this would increase productivity, reduce corruption and help the factory to become internationally competitive. The concept of spiritual economies makes it possible to see 'spirituality as an object of intervention, reconfiguring work as a form of religious worship, and inculcating an ethics of individual accountability and entrepreneurial responsibility' (Rudnyckyj 2009: 132).

Whilst it is illuminating to compare MLM and pyramid schemes to occult economies and prosperity religions, they are better encompassed within the concept of spiritual economies. The relation of the spiritual and the economic in the schemes is similar to that observed by Rudnyckyj in the Indonesian factory. Spirituality is encouraged through corporate power and for commercial interest. It is used as a technique of management for the purpose of motivating the workforce and forming their work ethics.

Multilevel Marketing in Aga: Amway

Amway was not the first MLM company in Aga, but it was the company through which MLM became widely known in the district. The company was founded in the United States by Jay van Andel and Richard DeVos, who launched their first product, a multipurpose cleaner, in 1959. Although the company has been accused of making deceptive claims, exaggerating the promise of wealth and exerting pressure on its distributors (see Chapter 2 for details), it can look back on a success story. Today, Amway operates in more than one hundred countries around the globe, with millions of distributors offering a range of health, beauty and household-related products. Since 2005, Amway has also established branches in Russia, which quickly became one of its largest and most important markets. Within its first year of operation in the country, Amway made sales worth of $100 million in Russia and after the second year, this figure had doubled. By 2008, Amway sales in Russia had reached $600 million and the number of distributors had grown to one million (Jones 2011: 142–43). As discussed in the previous chapter, there was a wave of registrations for Amway in Aga, starting around 2010 and reaching a peak in 2012. Amway became so widely known during this period that by the time I started my research in 2014, everyone I met in Aga was aware of their activities. For the vast majority of those who tried earning money through Amway, the scheme had not worked. They were neither able to sell enough products to make their business profitable nor to find more than a handful of people willing to register – unsurprisingly, given the sheer number of people who had made the attempt. Even Lobsan, the enthusiastic distributor who had first introduced me to Amway and who had been successful enough to rent the small office that I visited in 2011, closed his office in 2014 when the wave of registrations dried up and his business had become unprofitable.

Despite these circumstances, there are Amway distributors in Aga who are still enthused by the hope of making big money and who have not given up their mission to recruit people. They are led by the Tsyrempilovs, a retired couple from a small village in Aga's steppe, who have managed to reach the company's emerald bonus level. The Tsyrempilovs and their close relatives are Aga's Amway celebrities and they are the only people in the district Amway has catapulted into the promised world of dreams. Solbon and Oiuna Tsyrempilov participate in cruises in the Mediterranean Sea with Amway partners from other parts of the world that are paid for by the company and have an income that makes them quite wealthy by local standards. At the time of my fieldwork, the Tsyrempilovs also began travelling to other regions, mainly to Tuva, in order to attract new participants as this had become difficult in Aga.

Conversion

The Tsyrempilovs recruited people from different parts of the district and also from other regions where they went to advertise Amway. Within their own village, however, hardly anyone has accepted their invitation. Solbon Tsyrempilov told me that he could not understand why people were so shortsighted when I visited the couple in April 2015. Why would someone decline the offer to make a lot of money with his support? And why do his fellow villagers prefer working in miserably paid state jobs, why do they engage in unprofitable and strenuous farming and herding or do not work at all? Solbon knows that people talk behind his back about him and say that he is greedy for money, but he says that he does not care. For him, it is more important to support his family and to enable his children to live a life without financial troubles. Already in Soviet times, when he was employed as a driver for a collective farm, he worked additional hours in order to earn some extra money. After the farm had collapsed, he set up a small kiosk in the village where he sold chocolate and vodka. He worked hard in order to turn the kiosk into a shop supplying the basic needs of the villagers. When he first heard of Amway, he did not like the idea. He thought it was a scam. It simply sounded too good to be true. But the Amway distributor who visited the village several times to advertise the company did not give up on him. His wife joined first because she liked the cosmetics, he explained. It was Oiuna who convinced him that they should participate in one of the company's seminars. Solbon came along, unwillingly and certain that it would be a waste of time, but then the business trainer started talking about things he had never thought about before. He had always assumed that business meant buying products and selling them for a slightly higher price. At the seminar, he learned that it could be much more than that. He became curious, bought the trainer's books and started reading about business opportunities and about Amway. Solbon now says that the decision to become an active partner in 2010 changed his life. He still lives in the village where he was born and he is still running his shop, but his worldview and his attitude towards life are completely different. He now thinks positively, his health has improved, he has stopped drinking entirely and he is feeling simply great.

Solbon's example clearly shows a process or, perhaps more fitting, a moment of conversion. His is a typical story that I have heard from many MLM and pyramid scheme adherents. Initially, the idea of joining the schemes is rejected, but after a period of being exposed to missionary efforts, this attitude changes, often as a consequence of participation in ritual, i.e. a business seminar. Solbon's case also demonstrates the particular significance of the postsocialist experience for the impression the company could exert upon him. At the business seminar, he encountered what he believed to be 'professional' capitalism, a form of capitalism that was not petty trade for survival, but a form of capitalism that promised big money and opened up new horizons. From his perspective, people's unwillingness to join Amway can thus be easily explained in terms of their socialist mentality, which he believes to account for their ignorance with regard to profitable economic activity.

Pilgrimage

In July 2014, I went with the Tsyrempilovs and a group of fifteen other highly motivated distributors to an Amway seminar in Chita, the capital of Zabaykalsky Krai and the closest city to Aga. Amway organizes seminars in various parts of Russia, supported through the initiative of locally successful distributors. The largest seminar, a huge and spectacular event according to Tereshina's (2013) description, takes place once a year in Moscow. Seminars in other cities are held around the year and the most active distributors, like the Tsyrempilovs, participate regularly and travel great distances in order so to do. The seminars are expensive to attend and the fees, combined with the travel costs to venues, require considerable expenditure by participants.[1]

The hall of Chita's music theatre that had been booked for the event was almost full when we arrived. Music played loudly and hundreds of people, both Russians and Buryats who had come from different parts of the region, were dancing in the rows and the aisles under a huge Amway banner. Many were smiling, some clapping their hands to the beat of the music. Most people were dressed up, the men wearing suits and the women elegant dresses. The Tsyrempilovs walked up to the first row that was reserved for those on top bonus levels and hugged everyone they knew on their way. I sat with the other distributors from Aga who were not successful enough to be allowed access to the front seats. They pointed out the 'diamond' and 'emerald leaders', saying how beautiful and intelligent they are, and kept asking me whether I enjoyed the positive atmosphere.

What followed were two days of charismatic performance. These were mainly the testimonies of Amway celebrities like the Tsyrempilovs. With maximum enthusiasm, they told the audience about themselves, their way to Amway and about the company: 'What our company values is hope. And what many of you will receive here today is hope.

You were not invited here for the toothpaste. It is no longer necessary to advertise our products, our products sell themselves because they are unique. What you get here is an opportunity. Here, dreams are born.'

An essential part of their stories was always how they had come from rags to riches. These were stories of conversion, all cut from the same cloth.[2] At the beginning, there was darkness, debts and disbelief. They had been invited to join Amway, but did not want to listen, rejected invitations and decided to continue their struggle to make a living. But there had been a saviour, their sponsor, who had insisted with endless patience that they should join Amway. If this person had not been so caring and supportive, they would still be caught in their dull everyday life with all its debts and sorrows, without challenges and adventures.

Inbetween these narratives, a couple from Moscow ranking at the top of Russia's Amway hierarchy, clearly the most prominent guests of the seminar, presided over the event. Their speeches were followed by long applause, laughter and even tears. What they presented was chiefly a hymn of praise to the company and its unique opportunities. Moreover, the couple provided a glimpse into the glamorous lifestyle they had achieved through their merits: their holidays, their dream wedding and their material wealth were all demonstrated in films and photographs.

Those who performed praised Amway's marketing plan and Amway's products with their wonderful and miraculous qualities, be it the healing powers of the nutritional supplements or the stunning capacity of the cosmetics to make people look young and beautiful. The stage was not reserved only for those at the top of the hierarchy; rather, even small successes were celebrated. Sponsors congratulated their downlines for their achievements and encouraged them to continue, to overcome doubts and to cultivate a positive attitude towards the business.

Negative emotions, it was explained repeatedly, need to be pushed aside. To learn how to 'protect oneself from the stream of negative information' is key in order to become a successful distributor. In particular, shame is an emotion that needs to be avoided and newcomers have to train themselves to see selling and recruiting not as a shameful activity, but as something they can be proud of. Positive thinking, they emphasized, is a necessary tool for success with Amway.

Newcomers were also given the stage and told the audience about their first wonderful experiences with the products and about what they intended to buy with their future earnings. During the breaks, participants talked about their own personal experiences with

Amway, about their future plans and about the life of the celebrities from Moscow, frequently commenting on how much they enjoyed the seminar's emotional atmosphere and the company of friendly people. They asked the charismatic leaders for autographs or approached them with requests to have photographs taken together.

The people who had come to the seminar had been through different experiences with Amway. There were the celebrities, like the Tsyrempilovs, who had performed at many seminars and who were well known in the Amway community. A considerable part of the audience was made up of those who had only recently joined the company and who were attending the seminar for the first time. Some of them were not sure what to think of the company, sceptical as Solbon Tsyrempilov had been when he first heard about Amway, while others were enthusiastic to start working as distributors. There were also those who had been trying hard for a while and who had come to the seminar to learn from the successful distributors. After the seminar, one of my acquaintances from Aga, who had already been involved for two years, told me how important these events were for his motivation. He said that afterwards he always felt like one of those little wind-up toys that had just been set off again.

Collective travel and participation in Amway seminars across Russia are described as key events by active distributors, both for finding faith in the marketing scheme and for sustaining their faith. The seminars are described as spaces where positive thought and positive emotions are omnipresent and experienced collectively. Regardless of which MLM company or pyramid scheme they are promoting, participants state that these events help them to deal with doubt and enable them to keep enduring the everyday difficulties of their job.

Ritual

The Tsyrempilovs and several of their relatives who are also involved in Amway organize weekly business meetings in Aginskoe, which are small-scale versions of the above-described event. They come together in a school where they have an arrangement with the director to use the hall. Before the meeting, the distributors call neighbours, friends, acquaintances and colleagues in order to persuade them to come and listen. As Amway's activities are already well known and many people have no desire to hear again what they now regard as empty promises, this task is becoming increasingly difficult. However, in 2014/2015, the local Amway community still managed to find three or four new people every week who agreed to come to a meeting. Together with the active distributors of the Tsyrempilovs' downline, there were usually around fifteen to twenty participants. The meetings I attended always contained the same elements: a presentation of the Amway plan with the aim of demonstrating how much money can be made, followed by a presentation of the company's products, accompanied by narratives of their fantastic quality and accounts of new health, positive thought, happiness and wealth achieved through the company.

The event is held not only for the purpose of informing newcomers, but is also a training ground for distributors to practise their performance and presentation skills, as well as a way of coming together and enacting the Amway community. Distributors compliment one another on their new health and beauty achieved through the consumption of Amway products, and they congratulate each other for their achievements. However, they also express discontent if they feel someone from their downline has not tried hard enough to recruit more people. In this case, they remind the person that it is necessary to work hard instead of just sitting around and wasting time.

At the local level, the adaptation of the Amway logic to the local context is even more pronounced than at the large-scale seminars. MLM, its appeal and its image are framed in terms of the post-Soviet economic transformation, the current economic situation and local economic logics. At the meetings, recurring narratives present Amway as a glorious economic alternative and as a way to escape financial difficulties and the pressure of debt. The meetings are usually started with a number of questions to the newcomers: whether they are happy with their standard of living (the answer is mostly negative), whether they have debts (always positive answers) and whether they could use more money (the reaction often being laughter – of course, who does not need more money?). They continue with further questions, provoking the audience to imagine what they could have if they were rich, for example: 'What is the advantage of the network business [*setevoi biznes*]? Are there people here working as employees? If you are employed you live from one wage payment to the next, from one loan to the next and is there any chance to become rich and free? Or the chance to travel every year? No, there is not.' The conclusion is always the same: MLM would certainly be the best option for those present.

At local meetings, Amway representatives set the opportunities the schemes supposedly have to offer against the limited vistas people find themselves confronted with in their everyday lives. The reality surrounding people is deliberately contrasted with a world of dreams, in this case, wealth, freedom, security and travels. Thus, new fields of imagination are created: an imagining of a distant paradise that can be approached through the hard work of selling and recruiting for Amway.

Amway distributors in Aga claim to introduce a novel business model that has proved to be very successful in Europe and the United States. Solbon Tsyrempilov says that experts have shown that in a few years, Russia's whole economy will be based on MLM, and the increasing number of multilevel marketing companies in Aga is a clear indicator of such a development. MLM is presented as the economic model of global modernity. In Western market economies, so the narrative goes, MLM is a smoothly running and well-acknowledged form of business that has brought prosperity to many people. In Russia, on the other hand, the industry's image is problematic for the obvious reason that people had no experience with capitalist enterprise.

> Do you know how the negative opinion about the network business came about? In the 90s when the Iron Curtain fell, the Russians went to the West. They came to the West and saw that people are involved in network business [*setevoi biznes*], that they make a lot of money. They returned to Russia and copied what they had seen. But in our business the products must be of high quality in order to be recommended to others. The Russians came back and started selling whatever they found according to the network principle. And, of course, if someone tries the stuff at home and doesn't like it they won't recommend it and that's it. Therefore it didn't work here in the 90s. And then they offered the goods aggressively, bugging everyone, saying: Here, take this, take that. They offered it to people at their places of work and engaged in door to door selling. That's why there are so many prejudices against the network business today. (Amway meeting Aginskoe, July 2014)

There will be a time, Solbon Tsyrempilov promises, when people will understand that MLM is a solid business model and an entirely normal way of earning money. He reminds people that the same was the case with private trade in general.[3] Nowadays, he asserts, entrepreneurship is a respectable and, moreover, a profitable profession. And those who accepted earlier than others that it was necessary to accustom themselves to new market realities are today's successful businesspeople. People should remember this and join Amway before the niche is taken by others:

> Some people [who claim to have no time for Amway] are saying: I have a vegetable plot, I have cows. [Laughter] It is not profitable to have cows nowadays! In our village people have 20, sometimes 30 cows but they don't milk them and they don't drink their milk. They go to the shop [to buy milk], what do they need cows for? [Laughter] Pickled cucumbers cost 13 roubles. How much of them do you need? 'But this is self-grown' [people say to justify their activities]. This [attitude] is outdated. When I

> was in Spain, I didn't see any stables. It is only our country where every house has a stable with pigs and a greenhouse. We should let people do this who do it professionally.

Tsyrempilov portrays the local economy as outdated and offers Amway as a 'modern' way of making a living. He also tells people that they would have a great advantage if they would join Amway because it would offer them a new community, a community that supports each other, teaches each other and motivates each other. This community might overlap with established kin communities, since Amway is deliberately advertised as a 'family business' and often grows along kinship ties. However, the new community goes beyond a distributor's kinship network and provides a new network of people who share the goal to become rich and famous within their own world.

The ritualistic meetings provide a space for enacting and celebrating the community and praising its leaders. They are a way of collectively reflecting the problems many people in contemporary Siberia are experiencing, while offering hope to be able to one day escape these problems.

A Pyramid Scheme in Aga: WIC Holding

WIC (World InterContinental) Holding is the pyramid scheme that was marketed most actively in Aga during the time of my research. The company was founded in 2008 by Arkadii Sharov, a Russian who describes himself on his homepage as a professional businessman and an expert in network marketing (*setevoi biznes*). WIC Holding is running a fraudulent investment scheme, but claims to be a MLM company just like Amway. It pretends to operate a number of profitable business projects, among them a Christmas Market in Germany, a nightclub on Cyprus and an underwear sales business. WIC Holding invites people to become 'partners' (*partnery*) of the company and to buy shares for a minimum amount of 60,000 roubles (around $900). People are promised enormous returns on their investments, the amount depending on the number of investors they are then able to recruit.[4] The company also claims to be selling products that resemble those of Amway: nutritional supplements, cleaners and cosmetic articles. Partners receive a box of these products in return for their initial payment, which appears to be worth no more than 1,000 roubles (around $15). WIC Holding suggests that this gives them the opportunity not only to make money through their investment, but also to profit from the sale of these products.

The WIC Holding scheme was introduced to Aga in 2010 by a middle-aged woman, Ianzhima, and after about a year it was also actively supported by her sister. Both Ianzhima and her sister are local people who grew up in the countryside near Aginskoe. Hundreds of people have become shareholders of the company, but apart from the two sisters and a few people working in the office they have set up, none of the partners has received any significant amount of money. Even the most active participants who come to the office regularly and work hard to advertise the scheme have not received back what they have invested, let alone any profit. The company blames the delay in payment on a partner company that is responsible for the nightclub project and on the economic crisis following the sanctions imposed on Russia after its military invention in Ukraine. Partners are still hoping that they will receive their money, but, at the time of my research, it was already more than obvious that the pyramid was shaking.

The WIC Holding office that I visited frequently between July 2014 and July 2015 is located in the town centre, in a building with market stalls that has some office space for rent on its second floor. It is equipped with four small desks, a number of chairs, a television screen and a shelf on which the cosmetic products, nutritional supplements and cleaners the company pretends to be marketing are displayed. Thus, it strongly resembles the offices of MLM companies. On the walls there are pictures of the WIC founder Arkadii Sharov and of partners from elsewhere smiling under a shower of golden confetti. There are also pictures with local partners and their sponsors (they use the same language as MLM companies), who they accept as their teachers and supporters.

Proselytizing

WIC Holding encourages its partners to work according to a structured daily routine. The morning is reserved for making phone calls. These calls are made with the purpose of finding people who will agree to come to the office and to listen to the company's offer. This is difficult, perhaps even more difficult than finding people willing to come to the Amway seminars. People know about the scheme, they have been to the office and to the seminars organized by WIC Holding, and have either registered already or have turned down the offer. Like the Tsyrempilovs, the WIC Holding partners travel to other parts of the district and beyond in order to recruit more people. The company advises organizing meetings only in the office, as any other approach would give an impression of unprofessionalism to potential recruits.

In the afternoon, the so-called 'rendezvous' (*randevu*) should take place. This is the meeting with those they have managed to persuade to come to the office. An exact plan exists for how guests and potential investors should be greeted, where they should be seated and in what order the information about WIC Holding should be communicated to them. In the event that everything goes well, the guest stays for half an hour and listens to the explanations. Guests are first asked whether they have debts and could use more money. Next, they are encouraged to imagine what they would do with a lot of money. Then, they are introduced to the marketing plan, which suggests that it is very easy to make this money within a short period of time.

The presentation of the marketing plan is followed by an introduction to the products and accounts of their fabulous effects and healing qualities. Ideally, the guest agrees to come to a second 'rendezvous'. During the second meeting, additional information is given, including practicalities of payment. Ideally, the second 'rendezvous' should end with the guest's registration, including the agreement to make an investment. In reality, the whole procedure rarely goes this smoothly. Guests leave when they realize that they are being invited into a pyramid scheme or they sit through the first 'rendezvous', but never come to a second one. Yet even if they can be convinced to participate, there usually is a major obstacle: they have no money to invest. However, WIC Holding partners have an answer to this: people should simply take out a bank loan. They suggest that the returns will be high enough to pay back the debt, including the usually 25 per cent or higher rate of interest, in almost no time and still make a profit.

In the time between phone calls and meetings, partners are advised to learn about the company and to motivate themselves and one another. They study the company's website, the marketing plan and the ingredients of nutritional supplements, and they watch video clips with Arkadii Sharov. At least twice a week, they connect via Skype to one of the company's top executives. The latter live in different parts of Russia and provide business training to their downlines. The partners gather, greet the leader and then sit in order to listen to a charismatic speech about how to best make phone calls, about a new bonus programme or about how to successfully conduct a meeting.

The information they receive from Sharov or other people at the top of the pyramid is meant to be a form of guidance for local partners. Like Amway, WIC Holding organizes seminars in the cities and local meetings where the community meets face to face. Both in form and content, these events are very similar to those organized by Amway representatives that I have described above. Outreach is the declared goal of the events as well as of the partner's daily office work routine. However, proselytizing takes place in highly ritualistic ways and therefore is a key tool for strengthening a sense of community and creating a shared identity.

Imagination

Around ten partners come regularly to the office, largely Buryat women between their mid thirties and mid sixties. All the other people who have become partners do not work actively for WIC Holding. This means that they might have recruited a few people into the schemes, usually family members, but have stopped there. Either they could not find more people or they realized that a severe responsibility was linked to drawing people into the scheme. One of the women who comes to the office and pushes the scheme most actively in Aga is Tsyregma, Ianzhima's sister. Like several of her colleagues, she has worked in MLM before joining WIC Holding, but has not made enough money to justify the effort she has made. When comparing WIC Holding to Amway, it would be clear, she says, that the latter simply does not have as good a marketing plan as WIC Holding. This is why Amway does not work for most people. However, WIC Holding is different: 'In this company people can make real money.' With shining eyes, Tsyregma repeated this phrase like a mantra whenever I spoke to her. Tsyregma, like Solbon Tsyrempilov, often said to me that she could not understand why people are so reluctant to work for the company. They have debts, but do nothing in order to get out of it. People in the West would know, she explained to me, that it is necessary to make investments in order to make money. People in Aga, in contrast, have no financial literacy because they still have very little experience with business and finance.

Tsyregma never gave up hope of recruiting me into the scheme. Although I made it very clear from the beginning and throughout my fieldwork that I had no intention of joining WIC Holding or any other company, she never missed an opportunity to tell me about the fantastic opportunities that the scheme could offer or about the miraculous healing qualities of the company's products. As with other guests, she would make opaque calculations on a small calculator and on a piece of paper that were confusing even to herself. She spoke about numbers of people who could be recruited, about sums that needed to be invested, about percentages on these sums that would be paid back after a certain amount of time, about percentages on the company's bonus programme. She added and multiplied numbers, calculated percentages, converted sums from euros into Russian roubles and back until she ended somewhere with the conclusion that this was the amount of money which could be earned, exclaiming: 'Imagine, how much money…'

One day when I came to the office, Tsyregma explained the following to me:

> There is a group of capitalists, very rich and very powerful who are in control of the world's capital. No one knows exactly who they are but what is known is that they have their headquarters on Cyprus (this is also where WIC Holding is registered and where seminars for the top leaders take place). This group is called 'the closed group of capital' [*zakrytaia gruppa kapitala*]. The capitalists who make up the group employ several experts to work for them. Among these experts are administration staff, technicians, economists and also *seteviki*. One of the *seteviki* working for the group is Arkadii Sharov. And do you know why WIC is a Russian company? Because Arkadii Sharov is Russian.

After the financial crisis in 2008, Tsyregma went on to explain, the group of capitalists understood that 'network business' (*setevoi biznes*) would be the business of the future. The crisis had shown that 'traditional business' (*traditsionnyi biznes*) was no longer profitable. In contrast, Amway and other direct selling companies were proliferating even during the crisis and therefore proved that the network business model was a promising one.

At the first WIC Holding seminar that I attended in Aginskoe, I met Sanzhid, whom I knew from my previous period of fieldwork in 2011. Sanzhid, a man in his mid thirties, was running a small cafeteria in the town and was about to sell his business along with his car in order to invest the money into WIC Holding. He invited me to come to his cafeteria after the seminar and we went there together with Sokto, the only male partner who was working in the office regularly. Sokto is friends with Sanzhid and had recruited him into the scheme. Sokto, who has studied literature in Chita and is the father of three children, was dressed smartly, something that WIC Holding partners learn to be crucial for their success.

Sokto and Sanzhid were excited to tell me about the company. Sanzhid said that it was difficult to make money with the cafeteria, but life would become much easier within the next few months. The scheme, he said, would offer great opportunities. He had understood this at a seminar in Krasnoiarsk where he had travelled together with the other WIC Holding partners. There he had met people who had become rich through the company. He would now work hard, he said, to achieve what they had accomplished. He would definitely recruit his cousin, who was unwilling at the moment, saying that she did not have the money, but he was sure that he could persuade her.

Sokto was pleased with what Sanzhid explained to me and supported him by providing details. Amway had not worked for him, Sokto said, but this company was different because there was a lot of money in it. He did not want to live like his parents, who receive only a tiny pension and who have never been abroad. WIC Holding had given him the opportunity to travel to seminars in Krasnoiarsk, Moscow and even to Cyprus. Sokto was convinced that the company would have a spectacular future and would even expand to the United States.

Until late into the evening, Sanzhid and Sokto talked about people they could recruit into the company, lamenting that few people would understand what they could gain from participating in the scheme. They decided that they should speak to one of their acquaintances again, whose aunt might be willing to make an investment. Their acquaintance had registered, but was too reluctant to recruit actively. He still had a lot to learn, the two men agreed.

As these examples show, imagination is important in the context of pyramid schemes both in a temporal and in a spatial sense. The future is envisaged as a time of wealth, health and happiness. Calculations and numbers are used in order to demonstrate with seemingly scientific rationality that this can be achieved. To further support the idea of achievability, theories about capitalism's hidden mechanisms link WIC Holding to the sources of financial power. By establishing transnational connections to financial centres through personal links, money is imagined to become accessible. Thus, attention is diverted from where the money really comes from (the participants' friends and relatives) and the pyramid scheme is rendered a moral enterprise.

Conclusion

This chapter has suggested that companies like Amway and WIC Holding encourage the formation of spiritual communities for the purpose of cultivating a particular work ethic as well as for recruiting and motivating their salesforce. The techniques they use to achieve their aim strongly mirror forms of community formation in religious and spiritual movements. We could even imagine MLM companies such as Away, Avon and Tupperware as denominations of a common faith, and the pyramid schemes as radicalized splinter groups, essentially adhering to the same faith. They all share certain elements of ritual practice, morality and internal organization.

Unlike Rudnyckyj's (2009) example of an Indonesian factory, spirituality comes as an offer rather than as something to be learned as part of a formal job. The seminars, which are designed to teach people positive thinking, self-discipline and a particular work ethic, are voluntary. Spirituality may thus account for the appeal of the schemes and may actually become an important force in keeping people attached to the business. My examples demonstrate that distributors may value their work for the companies not only (or not at all) for material reasons, but also because they find it spiritually fulfilling. Although the spiritual side of the schemes rarely seems to account for their initial appeal, the power of positive thinking and the emotional experience of community tie people to the companies after conversion. In both the factory described by Rudnyckyj and the case of MLM and pyramid schemes, companies seek to cultivate a particular work ethic among their workforce. In contrast to the formal employment relations in the factory, in MLM and pyramid schemes, spirituality can become the primary cohesive force binding the network of people together. This is what makes them so similar to religious organizations.

It is important to keep in mind that the conversion my informants experienced was not in any sense *religious*. Most Aga Buryats are Buddhists and many also embrace shamanism. These religious commitments are not, in any sense, challenged by the schemes. MLM was neither associated with Christianity, nor did my informants see a tension between their religion and their involvement in the schemes. This mirrors the situation in Mexico described by Cahn (2011), where Roman Catholics did not see any reason to give up their faith when they joined the MLM company Omnilife. In Siberia, religious convictions were not an argument for opposing the schemes either. In contrast, the rhetoric of 'compassionate capitalism' and the idea of helping each other within and through the schemes seem to fit very well with Buddhist ideals of mutual support that are deeply anchored in Buryat society and morality. My findings resonate with Bernstein's (2013: 185–207) discussion of her encounter with a Buryat Buddhist lama who was involved in Amway at the time of her research. For him, individual entrepreneurialism and the idea of striving for greater wealth in no way contradicted Buddhist ideals. The lama saw Amway as a way out of poverty and as a version of desired modernity.

MLM and pyramid schemes blur boundaries between the religious and the economic, the spiritual and the rational, between possibility and practicality, and between reality and fantasy. They offer the chance to escape into a dream world, while at the same time constituting a practical attempt to make a livelihood. They allow dwelling in fantasies as much as acting upon the world in the here and now, for pursuing connection to the global while remaining loyal to the local. This is what makes them attractive, especially in times of uncertainty, but, as we will see in the next chapter, the everyday realities of selling and recruitment easily lead to disillusionment.

Notes

1. The seminar in Chita cost 1,000 roubles (around $15) and travel expenses for a day come to 1,000 roubles as well. This is considerable money in a region where the average salary is 16,044 roubles (around $240) and the average pension is 7,681 roubles (around $115) (Zabaikalkraistat 2013).
2. The terms 'conversion' or 'mission' are not used by distributors. I use them in this chapter as analytic terms.
3. During the first few years after the implosion of the Soviet Union, trade had a very negative image, as in Soviet times it had been condemned as immoral 'speculation' (Humphrey and Mandel 2002).
4. Profit depends on recruiting participants into the scheme. However, this is not always made entirely clear when participants advertise the scheme. They sometimes leave people believing that they can simply invest money and then wait for their interest to accrue.

4

Pyramids of Intimacy

Multilevel marketing and pyramid schemes are based on the recruitment of people with whom one entertains close social relations. Most people are drawn into the schemes through intimate social ties rather than through anonymous relations. This was true of the participants in the schemes whom I observed in Aga, and it is also a characteristic of these economic structures globally that has been widely noted in the literature (e.g. Cross and Street 2009: 9; Wilson 2004: Chapter 5). It is therefore rather surprising that neither the impact that the nature of these relations has on the schemes nor the question of how, in turn, the schemes affect social relations has received much scholarly attention or been explored in any depth by those who have noted it. The sparse literature on MLM and pyramid schemes focuses on the peculiarities of the industry and the social worlds of the companies rather than on sales situations and recruitment attempts. The appeal of the schemes has been mostly explained in the context of macroeconomic tendencies and processes of political transformation, whereas the role of grassroots social dynamics in their proliferation has not been considered. It is undoubtedly important to take into account large-scale developments and structures within which the schemes unfold, as I have done in Chapters 1 and 2. However, an exclusive focus on macroeconomic processes leaves out the microsocial environments within which the schemes operate. Moreover, it disregards the significance of their relation to local economic moralities for their development. The objective of this chapter, then, is to broaden and deepen my analysis by exploring the way in which the schemes work at a microsocial level.

The schemes are advertised to any person who the *seteviki* can think of and dare to approach with their offer. Every person who is contacted is a potential source of income to the MLM distributor or pyramid scheme participant as well as to their companies. Therefore, the schemes work inclusively, transcending boundaries of age, gender or ethnicity. The distributors are involved in various relationships with the people they invite: they may be relatives, friends, colleagues or more distant acquaintances. Although MLM and pyramid schemes grow along the lines of various social relations, I focus here on kinship ties, for the following reasons. First, kinship ties are of immense significance in Buryat society and, as I have shown in Chapter 1, they constitute an important basis for relations of material and monetary support in general. Second, my informants frequently pointed to the significance of kinship in relation to their involvement in MLM and pyramid schemes. Whenever I expressed surprise at the dimension of the phenomenon in Aga (often to explain why I had made it the topic of my research), people would have a ready answer for me: the schemes were proliferating because Buryats have many relatives who can be invited to participate. Indeed, the top local leaders of several of the schemes are close relatives. Amway, for example, is marketed most actively by Solbon Tsyrempilov, who I introduced in the last chapter, together with his wife, children, sisters, nephews and nieces. A focus on the role of kinship in economic life and in MLM/pyramid schemes in particular provides insight into local forms of economic reasoning, as well as into the rules and dynamics according to which kinship works in contemporary Buryat society.

The importance of kinship in Buryat society sits well with MLM's corporate ideology of encouraging 'family business'. Amway makes this agenda explicit in its marketing material and website, but I frequently encountered similar rhetoric in the context of other MLM and pyramid schemes. The proliferation of such rhetoric in Aga may well be the result of former Amway distributors trying their luck in other schemes. Amway (along with its imitators) promotes the idea that if the whole family cooperates, their scheme will be beneficial for all its members. Capitalism, it claims, can be 'compassionate', i.e. nonpredatory and noncompetitive. Telling people about Amway is a form of help because they are giving them the chance to earn money, and supporting those they have recruited with advice will be beneficial to everyone involved. Therefore, according to the Amway logic, the company is not only *like* a family, but it is ideal as a joint business opportunity *for* families. While MLM worldwide is clearly dominated by a female salesforce, Amway has expanded its range of products in order to make its business opportunities more attractive to men (Wilson 1999: 405). In Russia, it seems to have had some success with this approach, as several of the senior leaders I met at business seminars were couples. Nevertheless, the majority of those who are most actively pushing MLM and pyramid schemes in Aga are female, and often they were recruited by female relatives and / or have several female relatives in their downlines.

By growing predominantly along personal social ties, MLM schemes introduce market logic into the realm of the intimate and the domestic. As anthropologists and sociologists have widely demonstrated, nonmarket economic logics are entangled with and woven into market and monetary exchange in complex ways (Ferguson 2015; Gudeman 2008; Zelizer 2005). As these studies suggest, market exchange and nonmarket exchange are not guided by contradictory principles, nor are market relations and kinship relations separate spheres of social interaction. Therefore, rather than seeing capitalism as a determining logic or structure, we need to explore the social relations that generate capitalism and examine the intimate social networks through which capitalism is constituted (Bear et al. 2015).

While several studies have demonstrated the significance of kinship in the realm of production (White 1994; Yanagisako 2002), little is known about how kinship impacts distributive processes and marketing logic. As I have detailed in previous chapters, companies that operate MLM and pyramid schemes rely on the social networks of their distributors in order to grow and make a profit. Therefore, they are interesting cases with regard to the relationship between kinship and capitalism. In this chapter I explore the ways in which the social mechanisms of kinship enable the activities of MLM and pyramid schemes. In the context of the schemes, cooperation among kin may create something like a family enterprise, although not one of production, but rather in the sense of a little marketing or advertising agency. As I showed in the previous chapter, relatives run offices together and jointly organize meetings. However, this is only true for a small number of families, for whilst kinship dynamics support the growth of the schemes, I will show in this chapter that this does not always lead to the collective benefit advertised by the companies, but, more frequently, to social conflict and a collective loss of money. Companies exploit people's labour along with their resources and their social capital, but this happens in a way that still allows people to understand their activity in terms of support and to frame it in the language of mutuality.

A comparison to Deborah James' (2014) research on borrowing and lending in South Africa helps to clarify the approach I am taking in this chapter. James discusses the situation after apartheid when credit became available to those who had previously not had the opportunity to borrow. As in Siberia, this resulted in an increasing spiral of debt for many people. Interestingly, money is often not borrowed to satisfy personal consumer desires, but in order to invest in social and conjugal relations. Along with the accessibility of money through credit, new hopes and expectations developed (e.g. supporting less well-off relatives or paying for children's higher education) that are often out of proportion with the incomes people can earn. Thus, it is often communal obligation that drives people 'deeper into a hole' (James 2014). As James' example shows, the logic of mutuality and the desire to improve life, not just for oneself as an individual but also for the collective of which one is part, may benefit moneylenders and banks, and have a detrimental effect on local communities. The social logic to which James draws attention can also be found in the context of MLM and pyramid schemes. Particular capitalist relations introduced by companies or banks reach into the realm of mutuality and are able to extract profit from communities thanks to social expectations and obligations of kinship support.

In order to show how this interpenetration of capitalism and kinship has developed in Siberia, I begin by elaborating on the significance of kinship in Buryat society for economic life in order to lend greater depth to the understanding of local economic morality. The major part of this chapter will then focus on various facets of the complex relations between kinship and MLM/pyramid schemes. I will discuss how kinship obligation is drawn upon strategically by distributors to promote their schemes, how intimacy allows for effective advertisement, and how kinship relations are challenged and renegotiated through family members' involvement in the schemes. Thus, I wish to demonstrate how social organization constitutes pathways for economic action and, in turn, how MLM and pyramid schemes require integrating social logics into new economic realities.

Kinship and Sharing in Buryat Society

For the Buryats, kinship is of immense significance in terms of ethnic and personal identity. They trace their understanding of who they are and where they are from along the lines of patrilineal kinship. The Aga Buryats understand themselves to be descendants of their common ancestor, Khoridoi Mergen. The idea that the clan and the ancestors play a decisive role in the formation of the person can be found in a wealth of proverbs and legends (Tsydenova 2009: 82). To this day, the Aga Buryats identify with one of eight clans (*esige*) that are named after Khoridoi Mergen's sons: Khargana, Khuasai, Khubduut, Galzuud, Sharaid, Bodonguud, Sagaanguud and Khal'ban. To know one's clan and one's patrilineage is regarded as being very important, not only as a form of cultural memory but also to enable adherence to the rules of exogamy. People are considered to be too closely related to marry to the degree of seven generations. In families that are conscious of this tradition, genealogies are checked before marriages to ensure legitimacy. Apart from the patrilineage, Buryats are usually aware of a wide network of bilateral kin, extending at least to their grandparents' siblings and their descendants. Relatives beyond the third generation are considered to be distant relatives and relationships are usually not actively encouraged. Relatives come together as a group mainly at weddings and funerals, to which all close relatives should be invited. As close relatives may include an enormous number of people, making invitations to all impractical or unaffordable, it takes some knowledge and skill to invite the right representatives of a kin group and to avoid feelings of disrespect.[1] Apart from weddings or other rituals, including life-cycle rituals and religious rituals, people strive to maintain relationships with their relatives by visiting each other, for example, during Sagaalgan, the month of the Buryat New Year celebration. During the course of this month, elder relatives are visited and given presents as a sign of reverence. In the summer, children are often sent to stay with relatives, being told by their parents that it is important to get to know them. And as they grow up, young people are encouraged to cultivate relationships with their relatives by visiting them and helping them out. From early childhood, Buryats learn that their relatives are a category of people with whom one must be familiar and to whom one should be loyal and respectful. These cultural norms are manifested in kinship terminology and terms of address.

As described in Chapter 1, mutual support among relatives is thought of as a high moral obligation among Buryats. I have argued that such support is of crucial everyday economic importance. The idea of close economic cooperation among related households has been shaped within the context of the nomadic pastoral life of pre-revolutionary times, when the Buryats lived in small kinship units spread across a vast territory. Residential units of patrikin herded their livestock together, shared meat and supported one another with tasks that required labour exceeding the capabilities of a single household, for example, house building. Support from kin was also expected on occasions that involved great expense, most notably life-cycle rituals

(Humphrey 1998: 271–83; Sandanov 2004: 16–17; Tsydenova 2009: 79). Kinship ties were also important as a safety net in case of economic hardship. If someone needed urgent help – for example, if their yurt had burnt down – relatives would render assistance. One household would give building materials for a new yurt, another would provide clothes and a third would provide furniture (Linkhovoin 2012: 219). Interhousehold support was not conceived of in terms of debt. Provided that the person in need fulfilled his or her kinship obligations, relatives would not require them to return an equivalent of the material support they had received (Humphrey 1998: 282).

Collectivization brought about profound changes in Buryat social organization. New social units such as brigades, collective farms and party organizations were formed, regardless of the principles of kinship (Humphrey 1998: 268). People were forced to give up their traditional mobile way of life and to settle around a centre. As a result of the new structures of settlement, the local core of patrikin that used to live together broke up into several small households, usually living in some distance from each other. Several factors are likely to have stimulated this: settlement policies that deliberately aimed at breaking up kinship units, the allocation of house-sites by the committees of the collective farm or the organization where people were employed, and the right for each head of an independent household to obtain an additional smallholding. The result of this combination of factors was that families split up and that the local kin group dissolved as a residential unit as well as a unit of production (Humphrey 1998: 284).

Under the Soviet social order, a mutual system of support between relatives continued to be important, but it assumed a new dimension. The practical challenges of everyday life in the Soviet Union made a large network of kin, on whom one could rely, very valuable – perhaps most importantly as a buffer against economic uncertainty within the Soviet economy of shortage. Up until the 1950s, wages were quite unpredictable due to the weak organization of the collective farm economy. Moreover, food supplies were not guaranteed and shop shelves were often empty. Yields from private plots were subject to forced sales to the state, while the money earned was no real compensation for what had been given, especially in the light of constant shortages of basic purchasable food supplies. In this unstable economic environment, subsistence continued to be of great economic significance, in particular during the early decades of the Soviet Union. The small size of the new households required a supplementary labour force for occasions such as harvest, making households dependent upon each other. Under these conditions, a wide-ranging network of support on which one could rely became an essential coping strategy. This necessity, according to Humphrey, encouraged the cultivation of bilateral kinship relations (1998: 283–99).

Soviet ideology and politics had a major impact on the role of women in society. As the Soviet value system prescribed gender equality, women were given the opportunity to work in various jobs and to become active participants in political and academic life (Dugarzhapova 1987). Within the new social order, women often controlled household expenses, something that had previously been a male task. The new autonomy of women played a significant role in redefining the significance of certain types of kinship relations (Humphrey 1998: 287–88). This can be illustrated by the example of the Baldaev family whom I met during my fieldwork. Sergei Baldaev is from the Tunka region in Buryatia and his wife Urzhima is from Aga. They met in Aginskoe, where Sergei came in the late 1980s to seek job opportunities in construction work. After their marriage, they decided to stay in Aginskoe because Urzhima earned a good income as an accountant and, moreover, she had been given a house by the organization for which she worked. Sergei told me repeatedly that the decision to live in Aga was not the correct way of doing things. According to the tradition, they should have moved to his home: to Tunka. However, his wife's job had made it economically attractive to stay in Aginskoe and, as a consequence, it is mainly her relatives with which the family is now engaged in close reciprocal relations. As the example of this family underlines, a new mobility within the Soviet Union as well as the changed role of women in society have worked to transform traditional patterns of Buryat kinship without diminishing the significance of kinship as such.

The collapse of the Soviet Union brought about significant changes in Buryat social and economic life. Nevertheless, kinship remained crucial as a network of support, now concerned with balancing out the shortcomings of the capitalist economy, including repeated economic crises, increasing levels of debt and unemployment. Especially in the countryside, many people are dependent on subsistence farming, which usually means keeping a few cows or sheep and cultivating a vegetable plot. Therefore, at the time of the hay or potato harvest, kinship support is particularly important. Collective consumption remains significant beyond the single household. Domestic products, in particular meat, are sometimes sent long distances in order to share them with close kin living in the city or in other regions. I remember being quite puzzled as a student in Irkutsk when I learned that my Buryat roommates' parents were sending them potatoes and meat across distances of several hundred kilometres, often through travelling relatives. The degree of sharing depends very much on the family, but a high degree of sharing remains the ideal, regardless of how far people actually live up to it.

In the capitalist economy, money has assumed huge significance in social networks of sharing and reciprocity. This has been well documented for the African case (Ferguson 2015; Guyer 2004; James 2014) and it is equally true in Buryat society. Money constantly flows in small and in large amounts along kinship ties. Those who do not yet earn money themselves are supported as a matter of course. This is not seen only as the parents' responsibility: older siblings or cousins often make significant contributions. Giving and receiving money is not tied to age hierarchies and money may move in all directions. Whoever has money (and people know exactly who earns how much) is expected to share it with his or her closest relatives. These include parents, siblings and children, but may extend to cousins, aunts and uncles, depending on the emotional quality of the relationship, but also on the particular situation of the person in need of money – for example, on the question of whether there are other, closer relatives who might help. Who gives and who receives is dependent on many factors, including the financial situation of the giver, the need of the receiver and the wider circles of exchange in which they are involved. Sharing money does not mean that people with higher wages always give to those who earn less, but it is rather a question of who has access to money when someone else is in need of money. It may be small or large sums that are given, sometimes as a one-time transfer or in other cases as long-term support. It may be a few hundred roubles for a cousin who wants to top up their phone credit and has run out of money, it may be payments to a younger brother who studies at university, monetary support for an older sister who is building a house with her family, or contributions to paying off one's parents' debts. If the money is given as support, the purpose to which the money is to be put is normally clearly defined, in contrast to money disbursed as a present, for example, by a senior relative who comes to visit. Money may at times be given without having been requested and at other times it may be given upon request. It may be given without the idea of debt or it may be lent. Sometimes it is unclear whether the money will be returned or not. Sharing money is part of a system of support and it is seen to be a central kinship obligation.

In everyday life, shared consumption and monetary support is clearly something that is restricted to a circle of relatives with whom contact is emotionally close and frequent. Exceptions are ceremonial occasions, like weddings, when large groups of relatives gather and consume together. Money plays an important role at these occasions as well, but here giving is ritualized. Nevertheless, there are also obligations of support within wider groups of relatives outside ritual contexts. Relatives, for example, are always welcome to stay at each other's houses, even if they are not otherwise involved in close mutual relations of support. I know several cases where children, students or unmarried people lived with relatives for long periods of time, either because their own parents could not care for them, because they needed a place to stay near school or university, or because their relatives needed support in their households. Thus, kinship relations are also cultivated with more distant relatives, which may be significant in maintaining wider networks of mutual support.

Another type of support for which kinship relations were frequently activated under socialism and are again being drawn upon today relates to people's positions in wider society, primarily to their jobs. To have *blat* (e.g. a relative in a position of power) may make life a lot easier. It can solve problems or bring advantages, depending on the relative's place of work and on the level of their influence. This is true for Russia in general (Ledeneva 1998), but it could be argued that in Aga's clan-based economy, it is particularly significant. Although most Buryats consider education to be very important, a diploma is of marginal use in the search for employment. Good jobs are allocated through personal connections and kinship ties play a major role in this process. Moreover, workplaces may provide access to resources or services that can be offered to relatives under favourable conditions, meaning at a reduced price or free of charge. Having a wide network of relatives in different jobs is thus beneficial in terms of everyday coping, especially in times of high household indebtedness and in the face of a constant lack of money.

Networks of support are not limited to kinship ties, but include various other types of social relations. However, mutual recognition between relatives entails both obligation and entitlement to give or receive support if the circumstances allow. In practice, this social ideal often becomes a matter of negotiation, but despite major political, economic and social changes over the course of the twentieth century, kinship support in the form of goods, money and labour remains important economically. As we have seen, the patterns and shapes this support takes have been adapted to the economic challenges and conditions of the Soviet economy and to the capitalist market economy in turn. In the following section, I will take a closer look at the implications of these norms of mutual support amongst kin for

MLM and pyramid schemes. The focus of my interest is the question of how kinship relations affect the strategies used to market the schemes, in the dynamics that the schemes develop and in the consequences of their collapse.

Recruiting Kin

It is in the interests of *seteviki* to sign up as many people as possible with their companies, as their income depends to a great degree upon the number of people they can persuade to join their scheme. In training seminars, companies teach strategies to achieve this goal. The first step, newcomers are told, is to make a list of everyone they can think of. The list should include all their friends, relatives, colleagues, neighbours and acquaintances. The second step is to call these people and to encourage them to listen to what the company has to offer. The final step is to register them and to start working with them. For Buryats, relatives are a particularly large group of people who can be approached: They are familiar with even relatively distant kin, knowing how they make a living, where they live and through whom they can be contacted. Galina, one of the very few Russian distributors in Aginskoe, once commented that she is not very successful in her business because she does not know enough people. The Buryats, she said, have a great advantage because they seem to have an endless pool of relatives they can invite. Relatives are a promising source of potential recruits not only because of their numbers, but also, as I will show below, because mechanisms of kinship encourage their participation.

Pressure

During one of the training units held by the company WIC Holding, one of the largest pyramid schemes in Aga at the time of my research, one of the presenters explained to the newcomers how they should put together their list of people. She emphasized relatives as a group of people that should definitely be approached and invited: 'Relatives. We all have relatives, right? Nobody will say no. We all have, let's say … especially our clan is good. We have relatives on our mother's side and we have relatives on our father's side.' The speaker suggests that if the newcomers think along the lines of kinship, they will remember many people who they might approach with an invitation to join the company. The quote also reveals that relatives are thought of as a promising group of people from which to recruit, because it is difficult for them to reject the invitation.

Indeed, my close acquaintance Sergei felt that rejection was almost impossible. Sergei is the head of the household I have described above. He grew up in a small village in a remote region of Buryatia, where he worked on the collective farm before coming to Aga as a construction worker. Sergei is nostalgic for Soviet times and often explained to me how much better things had been back then. According to him, today people give up herding because they want to earn money and then they buy tons of things they do not need. Work, he believes, should be productive and it should benefit society. Sergei sometimes made fun of his distant relatives, the Tsyrempilovs, who are the wealthy Amway distributors introduced in the previous chapter. Only because they have earned a lot of money, they would behave arrogantly and think of themselves as important people. The Tsyrempilovs had come to their house when they first started to promote Amway in Aga in 2010. They told Sergei and his wife Urzhima about the company, about its marketing plan and about all the money they could earn. Urzhima registered, but Sergei did not want to have anything to do with it.

When the major MMM scheme flourished in Aga in 2012 (see Chapter 2 for details), thousands of people paid money into the scheme, among them Sergei's wife Urzhima. Like the other participants, she believed that an investment in MMM would bring them great returns. Sergei was not interested in the scheme and he did not want to participate. However, his wife, her cousin and their neighbour all joined MMM and they were enthusiastic about it. He described a situation to me when they were all sitting around the kitchen table in their house and the three women pushed him hard to pay his pension into MMM. He simply could not refuse, he said, and agreed to pay his small monthly pension of 9,000 roubles (around $135) into the scheme. A few weeks later, MMM collapsed and along with many other people, he lost his money.

As is obvious from this story, Sergei's wife Urzhima has a very different attitude towards the *setevoi biznes* than her husband. In principle, she remains open towards the idea, although she has had several negative experiences with both MLM and pyramid schemes. Urzhima thinks that she has simply been unlucky. She could have been successful in Amway, just like the Tsyrempilovs, if she had not fallen ill at the time, which prevented her from working sufficiently. Later she registered for another MLM enterprise, a Chinese company called Haogang that sells health-related products. In Haogang, Urzhima explained to me, she could have been successful if two women to whom she had sold a considerable amount of products on credit had paid the money they owed her. If people would only be honest, she said, the business would work. Urzhima also invested money into LBM, another major pyramid scheme (see Chapter 2 for details), but lost everything when the scheme collapsed. Despite all these experiences, she is still interested in learning about new business opportunities that could provide an additional income. Although she was curious about such matters, she was also annoyed by the calls she received from a distant relative in Ulan-Ude who kept inviting Urzhima to join a company she was working for. Once she even asked me to answer her phone and to say that she was not around. If she only had money, Urzhima said to me, she might register with the company this relative was working for, but she does not have the large sums required to join.

Urzhima's perception of the schemes, and her involvement in them, is typical of that of many women in Aginskoe. Investing money in the schemes is an economic strategy as much as a free time activity. She enjoys discussing opportunities for making money with her cousin, looking at product catalogues together or imagining what they could do with a lot of money. Like the vast majority of *seteviki*, she never took her activity very far, but she managed to register a few people. This meant a profit for the companies, but not for Urzhima. She spent a good deal of money to register for MLM and on products that she otherwise would not have purchased and, along with the people she had invited into the schemes, lost even larger sums in fraudulent investment schemes when they collapsed. She did not make a clear distinction between MLM and pyramid schemes, but would speak about the various companies in terms of their offers, bonuses, products and services. Pressuring her husband to invest his pension into MMM was certainly not tied to the idea of increasing her own profit. It would be wrong to reduce the motivation to recruit further people into the scheme to pure self-interest. Rather, it was tied to the optimism that an investment would bring high returns and that it would therefore be a reasonable decision to participate. There was a collective enthusiasm shared by Urzhima, her cousin and her neighbour that Sergei's money could multiply as well and that this would benefit the whole family. The basis of the conviction that the schemes could be beneficial for everyone is the assumption that they will keep growing and that those who join later will also be able to profit from their investment.

As this case shows, there need not be a tension between self-interest and mutuality. In order to understand the dynamics of the schemes, it is important to note the psychological significance of viewing them as an opportunity for everyone rather than as a mechanism through which a few benefit at the expense of many. As long as the limits of the system, i.e. the fact that it cannot grow indefinitely, is not acknowledged, it indeed seems to offer an opportunity to everyone. What is particular about the schemes is that they offer and encourage the vision of *collective* gain that resonates well with Buryat ideals of kinship.

Tricks and Trust

As discussed in previous chapters, the popularity of MLM and pyramid schemes in Aga reached such a degree that everyone had been invited to participate repeatedly. People were mostly annoyed by the invitations, did not want to hear about the companies and refused to sign up. In short, it was difficult to find people willing to come to the companies' presentations, let alone to register.

The difficulty of persuading people to come to the office and listen to the companies' offers sometimes leads *seteviki* who have decided to go about the business seriously to employ quite radical methods. They justify their methods by assuming a mission to educate people, to explain their chances and opportunities to them, and to help them achieve wealth and happiness. Companies teach the most effective practices of recruitment, such as not mentioning the purpose of the meeting when inviting people. Such information is not communicated in written form, but is passed down the inner hierarchy of the company, explained at seminars or during informal conversations in offices. The *seteviki* learn that they should bring those they invite into a situation where they have to listen. Many of my informants reported being in situations in which a friend or a relative had asked them to meet without telling them why, or had picked them up and taken them to one of the company offices without letting them know where they were going.

One of the most drastic means of luring people into their office was employed by the *seteviki* of WIC Holding. Badarma, an energetic woman in her mid fifties who at the time of our interview was actively working for WIC Holding, told me in an interview how she had been persuaded to join the company. Her cousin had told her about the scheme several times at weddings and other social events where they saw each other. Badarma was not the least interested in her cousin's stories at that time. She had a job in Aginskoe's administration and told her cousin that she was busy and had no time to work for the company. One day she received a call from her cousin, who asked her to come and help her. Her cousin said that she needed Badarma's advice ('Badarma abgai, pomogi mne tut eto, prokonsul'tirovat' menia'). Badarma agreed to meet her, although her cousin had not mentioned on the phone what sort of support she needed. They met and her cousin took her to the WIC Holding office, where she commanded her to sit down and to listen to what she had to say. Although she had been lured into the office under false pretences, Badarma stayed and listened to the marketing plan that her cousin expounded. Perhaps, Badarma said, she would not have become involved if this incident had not occurred shortly before her retirement. At the time, she was looking for ways how to pay for her son's education and her cousin assured her that WIC Holding would allow her to do so in the future. Badarma came to the office on several more occasions before she decided that she would work with them. She took a loan, paid the money into the scheme and started recruiting people herself.

I want to compare Badarma's story of how she was persuaded to join the scheme with that of Alima, an Amway distributor, to further illustrate how kinship obligation encourages the dissemination of the schemes. Alima, a woman in her early forties, lives in Chita and had been actively involved in Amway for about a year at the time of our interview. Alima had been invited to Amway repeatedly by different people, but, like many others, she had rejected the invitations. The reason, as she explained it in the interview, was that she was simply too busy running her two restaurants and therefore did not want to listen to Amway's business proposal. On one occasion, she was tricked into an Amway office by the mother of her daughter's friend. When she realized where she had been brought, she left immediately. However, a few months after this incident, her cousins came together with their sponsor in order to recruit Alima. Because it was her cousins, Alima explained, she was ready to listen to them ('Ia snachala poslushala tol'ko iz za togo, chto oni u menia dvoiurodnye kakby'). Although she had not intended to join the company, she registered under her cousins. Her cousins came at a time, she said, when she was looking for alternatives. Competition in 'traditional business' was becoming fiercer, taxes were rising and over the years it had become increasingly difficult to earn money through her restaurants. She began worrying about how she would survive financially once she was too old to run the restaurants. This, she said, was the reason why she decided to join Amway.

In several respects, Alima's account resembles that of Badarma. Both cases demonstrate the crucial role kinship relations played in familiarizing the women with the schemes. What Badarma's story indicates, Alima's story shows very clearly: it does make a difference from whom the invitation to join the schemes comes. Kinship bonds allow for setting up a meeting in intimate ways and also make it difficult to refuse to help or to reject cooperation. Neither Badarma nor Alima had any intention of joining the schemes; on the contrary, they were unresponsive to or even dismissive of invitations. Only when their relatives emphasized their kin obligation to help, as in Badarma's case, or when it was close relatives who made the invitation, as in Alima's case, did they agree to listen to the information about the companies. Interestingly, both women created an explanation that justified their decision to join the schemes in economic terms only in retrospect. However, this is not to say that they joined merely as a result of direct or indirect pressure. Motivations are complex and cannot be defined in negative terms only. Trust in the recommendations of their relatives and in the information they received might have been just as important to Badarma's and Alima's decisions. A relative is unlikely to be suspected of providing false information or of insincere intentions. On the contrary, a close relative will be assumed to act in ways that are in line with one's interests. Indeed, this may also be the case from the perspective of the person recruiting. As argued above, the form of the network business allows it to be conceptualized as an act of giving from the perspective of those who invite (giving an opportunity) as well as of those who are invited (giving support). This means that everyone involved can justify their activity as doing good, even though the schemes are ultimately likely to result in a significant loss of money for the group as a whole.

Conflict and Support

As we have seen, it is extremely difficult to attract new people to the companies and, consequentially, methods of recruitment are often aggressive. These may lead to the desired outcome, as in the cases of Badarma and Alima, but often they do not. Negative and hostile reactions are common and make the work of recruitment a great source of distress, not only for newcomers but also for experienced *seteviki*. The companies provide explanations for people's unresponsiveness to their offers. One explanation frequently given has been discussed in the previous chapter: the idea that people simply do not understand the opportunity that they are being given because they do not have sufficient experience with business, markets and finance. The other common explanation for negative reactions to invitations is people's experience with fraudulent companies and collapsed schemes, mainly with LBM and MMM in 2011 and 2012 respectively. All companies, regardless of whether they run MLM or pyramid schemes, readily acknowledge that pyramid scams are being operated in Aga in order to distance themselves from such illegitimate models. These explanations are important in reassuring *seteviki* that negative reactions need not be taken personally and that their work is purposeful and good.

I will now move on to discuss an example of how the attempt to recruit relatives into a scheme has led to conflict. I met Zhalma for the first time in 2011. At the time, she was working for a company called Global Trade System (GTS), which was selling health insurance through MLM. I remember her praising the quality of the insurance and the importance of good health insurance for people in Aga. Like Badarma, she had worked all her life in Aginskoe's administration and saw the company as a valuable additional source of income. In 2014, when I met her again, she had retired from her job in administration and was pushing a pyramid scheme called WinLevel. As in 2011, she was very friendly and supportive of my research, and I was therefore able to interview her repeatedly and get to know her more closely. Whenever she spoke about the schemes, she did so in an enthusiastic, almost fanatical manner, showing that she was absolutely convinced of the bright future of the *setevoi biznes*. When I learned that Zhalma was not working for GTS anymore, I asked her what had happened. The reason, she explained, was that the company had collapsed.[2] Zhalma told me that the Ulan-Ude leaders of the scheme had disappeared. According to rumours, they had moved to Moscow after the collapse. Zhalma had lost half a million roubles (around $7,523) in the scheme and was left with enormous debts. GTS was a scam and its leaders were fraudsters, she now understands. Zhalma does not blame her acquaintance from Chita who had invited her to the company because she is sure that her acquaintance had not been aware that it was a scam either. I asked her about the people she herself had recruited into GTS and who had also lost considerable sums of money. Some of them had been furious, she said. They had called her and asked her to help them get back their money. But what could she do? She did not know what had happened to the money and had lost money herself. Her colleague, who she had invited into the scheme, does not talk to her anymore. Her relatives still talk to her – after all, they are relatives, she said. But they are still dropping comments every once in a while, reminding Zhalma that she is responsible for their debts. In her view, however, people had given their money voluntarily and were therefore themselves responsible for their decision.

The new scheme that Zhalma is pushing is run by a Russian company that markets a service: it offers legal support for people who are unable to pay back their debts to the banks. The promise is to free people from debt by proving in court that the banks that provided the loans did not operate legally. The deal that WinLevel offers is that people pay a certain fee every month, the amount of which depends on their level of indebtedness, and the company's lawyers will work on their case. By recruiting further people to make use of this service, one can earn money. Zhalma is convinced that WinLevel is not a fraudulent company. As she has high debts herself, all her hopes of escaping the pressures that the banks are putting on her rest on WinLevel and its lawyers. She has been paying money into the scheme for several months, but so far nothing has happened to improve her situation. This, as the company had explained and Zhalma believes, must be attributed to the slow flow of information between the courts, banks and lawyers. Zhalma does not know anyone for whom the company's services have worked, but there is a video on the company's homepage showing a woman who gives a happy account of how WinLevel freed her from debt, which gives her confidence that it will work.

In October 2014, Zhalma went to one of WinLevel's seminars in Ulan-Ude. I met her shortly after her return to Aginskoe and was interested to hear about her impressions of the seminar. Zhalma said that she would love to tell me, but that she was not supposed to. At the seminar, they had been asked not to tell anyone details about what they had learned there, but instead to invite people to come to the next seminar themselves so that they could get the full and correct information about the company's activities. But she could tell me, Zhalma said, that the seminar had given her the opportunity to learn a lot about herself. It let her recognize that she is too reserved, that she needs to be self-confident about her own activity, to work harder in general, and that she needs to open up to people in order to be successful. During the seminar in Ulan-Ude, Zhalma had stayed at the house of her two cousins. She had told them about WinLevel and tried to persuade them to come along to the seminar, but the cousins had not been interested. After the seminar, she had an argument with them. Having realized that she was too reticent with people, she had decided to tell her cousins what she thought about them: that she finds it problematic that they do not earn their own money, but rely on their parents' and husbands' money. She had told them that they should give up hope of finding jobs in their field of expertise as this was highly unrealistic in Ulan-Ude. It was about time to contribute to their family's income, she suggested to them. One cousin had listened without comment, while the other cousin had become very angry. Zhalma did not want to go into further details regarding the conflict, but when I asked her whether she would stay at her cousins' house again when she next visited Ulan-Ude, she said that she might try to find another place to stay. However, she would certainly make further attempts to invite her cousins to join the company, she added. Zhalma thought that her openness had encouraged her cousins to reflect upon their financial situation and she was confident that they would understand that registering with WinLevel would be the best option for them.

Zhalma's case shows that the schemes may put a significant strain on kinship relations and provoke social conflict, in particular due to aggressive attempts at recruitment that may be very intimate and may be seen as insulting. The companies' training encourages distributors to imagine in what sense money could be important for the person they are inviting and to personalize their advertisement for the scheme. Distributors learn not to give up in the event of a negative reply, but to risk conflict by insisting on their cause.

A major source of conflict is not only the attempt to draw others into the schemes, but also the effects of their collapse, which raises questions of responsibility and demands to return money by the downline. As Zhalma's case illustrates, her colleague and her relatives did not (or not only) blame themselves, but also held Zhalma responsible for having invited them into the schemes with long-term consequences for their relationships. The collapse of a scheme may be psychologically devastating for those who have been actively involved. Not only are they being accused of fraud or of theft by people who have trusted them and joined the schemes in good faith, but they also lose their whole livelihood. For many, the collapse of the scheme they have promoted means that they are left with immense debts and a desperate need for material support. In this case, they are forced to turn to relatives for help and thus extend the consequences of their involvement to people who did not have anything to do with the schemes in the first instance.

Sanzhima, a teacher of economics at the small local university, found herself in such a situation. Both she and her mother have been involved in various pyramid schemes, which has resulted in the loss of a considerable sum of money. Like many people I met during my research, Sanzhima seemed to have mixed feelings about the schemes. She told me about fraudulent companies, about the loss of money, but also about new companies that sounded promising to her. Sanzhima had decided for herself that she would no longer try to recruit further people into any scheme. She wanted to invest because she believed this could be profitable, but did not want to draw further people into any scheme as she had realized that this involved a major responsibility. One of the company's representatives had told her that it was possible to simply make an investment and to get high returns without recruiting further people. In an interview, I asked her about the consequences of the LBM collapse and how it had affected her. Sanzhima had taken a loan in order to invest money into the LBM pyramid scheme. When the scheme collapsed, she had lost her money and her low wage was insufficient to repay her debt to the bank. She had to turn to her sisters for help, who had not known about her involvement in the scheme:

> Sanzhima: My sisters scolded us. 'Mom…ok, but you?', they said, 'what were you thinking? Such a great amount of money … You took a loan, without knowing … Seriously', they said, 'what were you thinking?' There was a conflict in our family … They [Sanzhima's sisters] gave us [the money] because what other solution was there? Otherwise the bank would have terrorized me. And my sisters gave us the money. And my mom also helped until she took a loan for this WIC [meaning a bank loan to invest into WIC Holding]. When she took the loan she could not help anymore. And my salary wasn't sufficient to repay the loan.
>
> Leonie: The money you borrowed in order to pay it into the LBM scheme?
>
> Sanzhima: Yes. And I had to take it from my sisters. I had to explain … When they learned … they didn't know that we were doing that and when I asked them [to give me money] they learned about it. Oh what a scandal that was. How they scolded!

Sanzhima had a conflict with her sisters because they were brought into a position where they had to help her. Although they had not participated in the scheme themselves, they were affected by its collapse because of kinship obligation. The accusation of being responsible for the loss of money may therefore come from various sides: from the people the participant has drawn into the scheme and from those who have to support the participant who has lost everything. Thus, kinship support may both enhance the growth of the schemes and ease their collapse for participants. Combined with the morality of mutual support and Russian legislation that until October 2015 did not make it possible to declare personal bankruptcy, the logic of pyramid schemes could draw whole groups into financial disaster.

Conclusion

Kinship is of immense significance for economic life in Buryat society. Kinship relations determined economic patterns in pre-revolutionary nomadic pastoralism and they continued to be important in terms of coping in the socialist economy of shortage. In this chapter I have shown that the significance of kinship has not diminished in the context of capitalism; on the contrary, intimate relations of mutual support play a significant role in the free market. Kinship relations have an impact on the nature of commerce, on economic considerations and on flows of money (cf. Zelizer 2005). With regard to MLM and pyramid schemes, I have shown how the local moral economy shapes the adaptation of a whole industry and its fraudulent cousin. Kinship relations are important in the strategies used to market the schemes, in the dynamics that the schemes develop and in the consequences of their collapse. MLM and pyramid schemes, in turn, may unsettle relationships, problematize them or lead to new forms of cooperation through shared ideology and within new communities. Capitalist relations of production, and indeed of distribution, then, are not necessarily the impersonal and formalized relations between actors in an anonymous market theorized in economic textbooks, but are deeply embedded within intimate settings and social relationships (cf. Granovetter 1985; Gudeman 2008).

I have argued that the dissemination of the schemes is supported through kinship relations in various regards. The sheer number of kin Buryats usually know provides a broad pool of people who can be approached in intimate and sometimes radical ways. But it is also the nature of kinship relations that provides a fertile ground for the dissemination of schemes. Within intimate relations and contexts, pressure can be exerted more directly and, perhaps, more effectively. Social proximity allows recruiting ruthlessly without much risk of a total rupture of the relationship and without experiencing the shame associated with such behaviour in a wider social context. On the other hand, close social relations and kinship in particular are often based on trust. The information about the scheme is believed more readily if it comes from a familiar source. Monetary reward is imagined and people are often not clear about what it means to become involved. The often vague information people are given about the chances of profit, the sources of the money and the stability of the enterprise is usually accepted and rarely questioned. Thus, emotional factors and social dynamics seem to play a more important role than calculative rationality in the decision of whether or not to join the schemes. I suggest that in a context in which kinship and everyday mutual support is of high moral significance, the schemes flourish particularly well.

A focus on kinship relations shows that it is not merely the dream of big money, greed or self-interest that makes people commit to MLM and pyramid schemes; rather, participation may well be envisaged as a collective project. Such imaginings are supported not only by the pyramid structure of the schemes but also by the companies' rhetoric, which encourages distributors to think about their activity as a form of help. Thus, the schemes provide an example of how individual interest is reconcilable with the idea of mutuality and sharing by imagining it as part of a collective project that will be beneficial to everyone. The fact that growth is limited and that it is only a small group of people who will ultimately profit is neglected. The rhetoric of possibility along with that of mutuality displaces reality. An analysis of the schemes from the perspective of kinship relations reveals a widespread and powerful conceptual strategy to provide a moral justification for capitalism as an economic system.

The involvement of whole groups of relatives in many cases results in a collective loss of money. Naturally, this is more significant in the cases of pyramid schemes where large sums of money are at stake. Not only do those who believed in the possibilities of the pyramids lose their money, but those who have to support them are also negatively impacted. Kinship here comes to be important for the security network that it has always provided. However, it is not only pyramid schemes that can rebound on the system of mutuality built around kinship. MLM companies may also profit from exploiting the labour of those who are hoping to earn money. Their largely unremunerated work consists in finding further people who will also give money to the company, be it through membership fees or the purchase of products. As this chapter has shown, rules and mechanisms of kinship obligation and solidarity may lend themselves to exploitative structures, with problematic effects for the whole community. As a result, the claim to be doing good by doing well can be difficult to sustain. One way in which people are able to maintain belief in the company they are serving, as well as belief in their own integrity, is through attributing a heightened significance to the products they sell. The role of products in MLM and pyramid schemes will therefore be the focus of the next chapter.

Notes

1. Invitations are therefore usually organized by the parents.
2. GTS had been supported by politician Aleksei Krasnopeev, a deputy of Buryatia's parliament (Baikal-media 2005).

5

Pyramids and Their Products

MLM companies in Aga offer a range of products, most of them health, household and beauty-related. This focus mirrors the worldwide trend in direct selling, with 32 per cent of sales made in the 'Cosmetics and Personal Care' product category and 34 per cent in the 'Wellness' category (World Federation of Direct Selling Associations 2018b). As noted previously, some of the companies that run pyramid schemes offer the same products as MLM companies, for example, day care crème, nutritional supplements and herbal tea. These sales do not form a significant part of the business model and their primary purpose is to veil financial fraud. Other pyramid schemes offer services, mostly insurance services or legal protection, as part of opaque investment programmes.

The proliferation of the schemes, then, is associated with the distribution of a range of goods and services. Although recruitment is the primary preoccupation of the *seteviki*, sales (in the case of MLM) or what look like sales (in the case of pyramid schemes) must happen alongside recruitment if the pitch is to be credible. A particular feature of the MLM industry, which has been the focus of much criticism, is that the distributors sell mainly to themselves. Companies put immense pressure on their salesforce to consume its products regularly. Similarly, the companies running pyramid schemes exert pressure on those who have already signed up to buy further products and services or to upgrade services, which, in the schemes I have studied, were linked to investing more money. As a result, the people who are already involved in selling and recruiting are, at the same time, the most important consumers of the industry's products and services.

A focus on the products and services marketed through MLM and pyramid schemes can add much to an understanding of the social dynamics that the schemes develop. In this chapter, I begin from an understanding of consumer desires as being inherently social rather than located in the individual (Douglas and Isherwood 2003). Instead of seeing consumption as mere self-realization, I am also interested in its capacity to generate social relations. What I want to explore below is the question of how people come to see the goods and services marketed through a very particular retail channel as valuable and worth spending considerable amounts of money on. To this end, I explore how these products are embedded in various relational contexts and 'regimes of value' (Appadurai 1986). Appadurai's important essay on 'Commodities and the Politics of Value' offers a useful framework for thinking through my data as he draws attention to the creation of an object's value through its circulation. Moving beyond the Marxian preoccupation with production (Meillassoux 1981; Sahlins 1972) Appadurai takes as his starting point Simmel's assertion, more precisely his idea that objects have no absolute value, but that value is generated through exchange. Through his focus on the 'social life of things', Appadurai allows us to leave behind stark distinctions between capitalist and pre-capitalist societies (Polanyi 1944), and between the commodity and the gift (Gregory 1982). Thus, he enables us to reflect on the value of a commodity, not only in the theoretical context of anonymous capitalist markets, but also in the context of the local moral economy, domestic spaces and relations through which consumers encounter the object.

The commodities that are brought into circulation through MLM are produced in various countries and are distributed across borders to national and local centres. They are global brand names, sold in different currencies and market environments. Although a crosscultural comparison of Avon cosmetics or Amway cleaning materials might be fascinating (cf. Watson (2006) on the significance of the McDonald's brand in several Asian countries), this is not what I am concerned with here. Instead, I wish to explore the value attributed to the objects within various *local* contexts of economic reasoning. I will look at the goods and services marketed through MLM and pyramid schemes within three different but overlapping socioeconomic spheres in order to show how the value of the commodities is constituted and how it is perceived by different consumers.

The first section of this chapter discusses the commodities' market value. Here I want to look at the appeal of the goods and services in the context of the local consumer environment. For this purpose, I first explore the significance of consumption, shopping and brand names in the postsocialist rural market, and then show how the commodities marketed through MLM and pyramid schemes relate to this particular environment. In the second section, I look at the value that the goods and services assume within the Buryat economy of support. Here, I focus my discussion on the relationships through which the products are sold or circulated. This extends the previous chapter's discussion of the significance of kinship ties for the proliferation of the schemes and makes apparent that a purchase based on pure desire for the commodity is rather exceptional. Instead, the consumption of goods and services is deeply embedded in an exchange of favours and assistance that is part of, and often forms the basis for, market activities. In the third section, I deal with the products as part of the economic microcosms of the schemes themselves. In this context, I argue, the commodities assume supreme value for *seteviki*, as objects with superpowers and as symbols of hope.

Consumption during and after Socialism

In order to develop the argument regarding the significance of commodities to the relationships in which MLM and pyramid schemes are embedded, it is necessary first to provide a picture of the recent changes in the material environment and ideologies of consumption that have been experienced by people in postsocialist societies generally and in Aga in particular. Since my focus is a different one, what I present in this section is merely an outline sketch, limited to the background information I conceive as most useful to understanding the appeal of MLM and pyramid schemes products and services in a postsocialist consumer environment.

In contrast to capitalist economies, the Soviet economy, preoccupied with production and industrialization, attributed only marginal significance to consumer interests and desires (Verdery 1996: 26–27). The idea of tailoring products for individual consumers was opposed for ideological as well as for pragmatic reasons. Instead, there was an attempt to rationally determine universal basic needs and to meet them by means of standardized mass production. By controlling consumption, the socialist state intended to create and maintain an alternative to capitalist consumerism that, from the Soviet perspective, was to be rejected for its reliance on exploitative modes of production and the resulting unequal distribution and waste of collective resources, as well as the unacceptable methods it used to fuel desire for things people did not need (Fehérváry 2009; Oushakine 2014).

The task of regulating consumption proved to be a significant practical challenge and shortages of consumer goods were an everyday reality under socialism. Long queues and empty shelves have therefore become emblematic of life in the Soviet Union. Whilst it is undeniable that certain goods were in insufficient supply and certain desires remained unfulfilled, recent studies of Soviet consumption (Fehérváry 2009; Klumbyte 2010; Oushakine 2014) suggest moving beyond the influential paradigm of the Soviet 'economy of shortage' (Kornai 1992). We need to remember that the notion of scarcity is relational and has been constructed from the perspective of a society living in abundance (Sahlins 1972). With regard to the Soviet Union, the Western picture of the deprived Soviet citizen was also ideologically charged and popularized for political reasons. This picture seemed powerfully convincing in a capitalist consumer society, which promoted an ideal of moving ever closer to fulfilling people's endless desires. Fehérváry (2009) makes us aware that while the idiom of shortage is valuable for understanding the mechanisms of the Soviet economy, it limits the analysis of socialist consumer culture. It precludes the exploration of how the material world shaped Soviet identities and prevents us from seeing the effects of consumer practices on the economy. Moreover, the emphasis on goods that were in short supply obscures the fact that there was also a 'socialist abundance' of vital goods and services such as health and childcare, heat, subsidized food and drinks, and holidays (Fehérváry 2009: 432–35).

During the socialist era, most goods that were not allocated through the workplace or produced on private plots of land were bought in state shops (Humphrey 2002: 44). In Aginskoe, two shops were being operated in the 1980s, one selling household supplies and the other selling food. Shops in nearby mining towns were better equipped and people from Aga either went there to buy what was not available in Aginskoe or took a small aircraft to the closest city, Chita, which was easily affordable at that time. In order to obtain scarce consumer goods, people often relied on the informal economy, most notably on personal networks of acquaintances. People needed not only information about when and where desired commodities would be available, but also people in positions of relative power such as shop clerks who could 'reserve' things for them in exchange for a tip or a favour (Humphrey 2002: 44; Ledeneva 1998; Verdery 1996: 27).

The Soviet stance towards consumption was reflected in standardized shop names with uniform window displays, institutional shop interiors and simple packaging of goods (Fehérváry 2009: 438–43). The whole shopping experience, so Humphrey (2002: 45–46) argues, reflected that it was the state allocating goods to its citizens rather than customers choosing what they wanted to buy. The customer was separated from the things not only through long queues but also by means of the architecture of shop interiors. Goods were stored on shelves behind counters and could only be accessed with the assistance of clerks. However, whether they were willing to provide assistance depended on their grace, mood or relationship with the customer. Humphrey gives a lively ethnographic description of how people could be turned away in a food shop if they had not brought their own wrapping paper for butter, how the shop clerk could refuse to give them the piece of meat they wanted and how if they did not have the exact sum for payment, the person at the cashier desk who often sat on an elevated platform could complain or throw down sweets as change to the customer.

Soviet citizens attributed particular value to Western goods and brands. There were state shops where Marlboro cigarettes and Pepsi could be purchased for dollars. Access to these shops was restricted to those privileged people who were allowed to possess foreign currency (Lemon 1998: 40). While the packaging of Soviet produce was simple, Western brands such as Colgate or Palmolive were sold in Hungarian state shops in elaborate gift wrapping and to significantly higher prices than comparable Soviet goods (Fehérváry 2009: 440). As Yurchak (2006) shows, Western (*firmennyi*) clothing was extremely popular in Russia during the 1980s. American Lee or Wrangler jeans could be purchased on the black market for prices that came close to the average monthly salary of Soviet citizens. Students used empty Western liquor bottles or beer cans to decorate their dormitory rooms, they carried plastic bags with English print and sewed Western labels on sweaters and jackets. Through particular styles of consumption, so Yurchak argues, a link to an 'imaginary West' was established. Establishing this link did not even require 'real' commodities: the symbolic power of empty packaging and fake brands could create a connection to an imaginary elsewhere. The circulation of Western symbols was not a sign of political protest, nor was it incompatible with socialist values. Rather, these symbols were reinterpreted in local terms and, perhaps paradoxically, they were both enabled by the socialist project and constitutive of late Soviet culture (Yurchak 2006: 158–206).

Although the Soviet system established limits to consumption, it would be wrong to assume that *Homo Consumens* (Bauman 1976: 102–3) can exist only in economic contexts where consumer demand is the basis for economic growth (Fehérváry 2009: 441). As studies of Soviet consumption show, not only was there an elaborate official ideology tied to the question of consumption (Oushakine 2014), but also Soviet consumers themselves creatively shaped consumer worlds, whether through making Soviet products what they wanted them to be or by finding access to the consumer goods they desired through informal means (Yurchak 2006). Certainly, people did not always get what they wanted and desires remained unfulfilled, but, nevertheless, a shopping trip could constitute entertainment (Fehérváry 2009: 441).

With the transition to the capitalist economy, the pursuit of commodities continued, but now the challenge was not to find the goods one desired, but to find them at an affordable price. With the disappearance of 'socialist abundance', money was required to pay for education, healthcare and other necessities previously provided by the state. Thus, as described in Chapter 1, the new object of scarcity was money. Masses of commodities became available, but, especially in the first decade following the collapse of the Soviet system, there was little work, massive inflation and, for most people, no means to purchase anything beyond their subsistence needs. With the new permeability of borders, a wealth of novel commodities swept into the postsocialist market. In Aga, thanks to its proximity to the border, a mass of products (including clothing, building materials, household articles, technical devices, and fruit and vegetables) was imported from China. Traders from Aga began commuting to the border town, Manzhouli, and brought back items to sell in order to make a living. The quality of the commodities that appeared in Aga's improvised outdoor markets was unknown at first. People reported being impressed by all the colours and cuts of the Chinese textiles and clothes. Soon, however, they realized that these imports were largely of low quality and still today people complain about fruit without taste, clothes that tear quickly and electronic devices that break after a few months.

As in other parts of the former Soviet Union, there is nostalgia for Soviet commodities (cf. Klumbyte 2010). Food is said to have been natural, without preservatives and additives, and clothes are remembered as unfashionable, but of solid quality and durability. I frequently observed during my fieldwork that when people wanted to judge the quality of a product (for example, the gifts I brought), they checked where they had been produced. If the product was 'made in China' or was known to have been imported from China, it was assumed to be of low quality. In the local markets, traders explicitly advertise products to their customers as *not* imported from China, but as 'our Russian production' (*nasha rossiiskaia produktsiia*). Despite the negative image of Chinese imports, they remain popular consumer goods both because of their low price and because not much else is sold in Aga. The quality of commodities was something in which people in my field site took a vital interest and that they frequently discussed. When I first came to Aga, I was puzzled as to why people kept asking me where the commodities in German shops were produced. Only later did I realize that for them, the origin of a product is a crucial indicator of its quality and value. Brands or particular shops rarely appeared in discourse as markers of quality; rather, it was the site of production that was thought to be a vital referent in this regard. As I will show below, MLM was able to transcend this focus on place of manufacture because, thanks to personal advertisement, MLM products could quickly be established as brands.

With the collapse of the Soviet system, the consumer environment not only changed as a result of the influx of new commodities, but new spaces of trade and consumption also emerged (cf. Diatlov 2000). The new traders in Aga sold their goods in the improvised open-air market in the centre of town or in their homes. Only from the late 1990s did they begin moving into small shops or to the newly built indoor market where most are located today. Despite the gradual establishment of new trading sites, domestic spaces remain important for selling, in particular when people engage in trade only occasionally. It is not unusual that someone sells a few pieces of jewellery they have brought from Chita, shoes they have ordered online in large numbers or herbal tea that an acquaintance has brought from China. Advertising commodities to friends or relatives is therefore nothing extraordinary in Aga and does not only happen through MLM and pyramid schemes. Traders sometimes offer commodities directly to their acquaintances, but sales may also be mediated via personal networks; for example, people might say 'I know someone who sells beautiful jewellery, you should have a look at it' or 'Do you want to buy some of the very good, cheap meat that my friend sells?' For the seller, occasional trade may be a source of extra income (often it is mothers or pensioners who engage in it) and for the customers, it is an opportunity to buy something that may not otherwise be available in the district or may be more expensive if they purchase it from someone they do not know. As in Soviet times, commercial transactions often involve personal relationships, regardless of whether they take place in domestic spaces, public environments or markets. Loyalties and favours play a major role in trade and personalized trade relations are seen to be profitable for both sides – for the traders, it provides a guaranteed clientele, and for the customers, it allows access to reduced prices and credit.

A factor that had a major impact on patterns of consumption in post-Soviet Russia was the increasing availability of consumer loans. From 2010 onwards, banks granted considerable sums to almost anyone who asked for a loan. Consumer loans had been available since the early 2000s, but before 2010, they were difficult to access. Applications were bureaucratically complicated and in order to be successful, people needed to prove that they had a sufficient income or collateral. Banks simplified the procedure at a time when the economic crisis of 2008 had died down and wages were rising. As a local bank director explained to me, the economic upswing made banks confident that lending was profitable and it made loan takers confident that they would be able to return the money they borrowed. A friend of mine who grew up in Aginskoe and left the town in 2008 to study at university in Irkutsk told me about her impression of Aginskoe when she moved back, six years later. There were considerably more new cars in the streets, she said, many of her relatives and acquaintances had renovated their houses, young people were wearing expensive fur boots that had always been regarded as a great luxury, and every family owned several phones, tablets and notebooks. This new living standard may have been partly be the result of a general improvement in the economic situation in the district from the late 1990s, but it had certainly also come at the cost of tremendous levels of household indebtedness.

The availability of consumer credit coincided with the extension of mobile phone and internet coverage to the district and with the booming demand for new and expensive technologies. 'How could we ever afford a nice phone without a loan? Our pensions and wages are too low to buy them' is the logic with which people explain their decision to take loans. The availability of credit is recognized as being a curse as much as a blessing. People have realized how difficult it is to handle debt, in particular in the light of high interest rates that result in the rapid growth of sums of money owed to the banks. Although there is an awareness of the problems associated with debt, people continue taking loans, partly because they are caught in the vicious circle of debt and partly because consuming on credit quickly came to be seen as entirely normal. Everyone does it and it might even cause puzzlement if someone were to reject the opportunity to take out a consumer loan.

However, consumer desires and the definition of status via consumption are only part of the explanation for the high level of loans people have taken. Banks and traders certainly had their interest in attracting debtors, and strategies to achieve this. This may be illustrated by the account of Galina, an elderly Russian lady who told me about her shopping experience. A year or so before our interview, she went to the shop to buy an antenna with one thousand roubles (around $15) in her wallet. In the shop she remembered that she also needed a kettle. The two items together cost more than the thousand roubles she had in cash, so she asked the shop assistant whether it was possible to take out a loan for the cost of the two articles. The few shops in Aginskoe that sell relatively expensive items, such as jewellery and electronic devices, have agreements with banks that allow them to sign contracts for consumer loans directly in the shop. Small signs on every shelf in these shops read 'Yes, get credit' ('Da, beri kredit'). Galina was told that she would have to spend a minimum of 3,000 roubles to qualify for credit. The shop assistant suggested that she should buy a further item, perhaps a vacuum cleaner. Her purchase would then exceed 3,000 roubles, enabling her to obtain a loan. Galina had not intended to buy a vacuum cleaner, but agreed to the deal and bought the three items. As this case shows, it was only partially consumer desire that persuaded Galina to take out the loan. It was the combination of the strategies of the bank and the trader with her lack of money that accounted for the decision to take the loan and buy something she initially neither wanted nor needed. Accounts like this demonstrate that consumer demand does not emerge miraculously or naturally, but that it is created. In order to understand people's decisions to take out loans or to use credits cards, we have to look closely at the interest of financial institutions and at their strategies of marketing financial products (cf. Guseva 2008: 37–44).

The transition to a market society created a new consumer environment. There was an influx of commodities that were offered to the consumer in novel ways by people who were largely inexperienced in commercial trading and in trading in new spaces, such as improvised outdoor markets and private shops. The shopping experience changed along with the logic of payment. Debt became an everyday reality in a context where commodities were needed and desired, but money was scarce. This development was supported by banks and traders that granted credit in order to encourage people to spend money. As a result, patterns and social logics of consumption shifted, as did the relationship between people and commodities. While Soviet era commodities were sometimes difficult to obtain, commodities are now readily accessible and are sometimes forced upon the consumer. Whereas it used to be a favour to grant access to a commodity (as, for example, shop clerks did when they reserved commodities for their acquaintances), today the purchase of a commodity (that is, the willingness to give money to a trader who needs to earn money) can be a favour. In the following discussion of the commodities marketed through MLM and pyramid schemes, I seek to illuminate the mechanisms of this new consumer environment in more detail.

Personalized Marketing

In the late 1990s, MLM companies began offering their goods for sale in Aga. There were several features about the products and the ways in which they were marketed that set them apart from the commodities offered by means of what *seteviki* call 'traditional' trade. My objective in this section is to demonstrate how the cleaning materials, cosmetic articles and other MLM products, as well as the services offered through pyramid schemes, came to be seen as valuable within Aga's postsocialist market.

Most of the traders who began commuting to China or to Russian cities in the 1990s in order to purchase goods for sale in Aga had no previous experience in doing business. For them, business meant selling commodities at a higher price than the price they had paid for them. Trading was often unorganized and small-scale, and as a result of the stigma attached to private trade in the Soviet period, it retained negative connotations. Many people started trading because economic condition forced them to find ways of earning money where few other opportunities were available (cf. Humphrey 1999: 31). MLM stood out as a distinctive form of trade from the very beginning because, unlike other petty trade in Aga, it was linked to large-scale corporate business. The distributors had contracts with companies that organized trade in a particular way. The companies managed the delivery of the goods and issued guidelines as to how selling should take place, which strategies should be used and how products should be advertised. Moreover, they offered motivational seminars where their distributors were trained to work 'professionally'. During seminars, the distributors were encouraged to study facts about the companies, its goods or services and the art of marketing. They learned how to offer commodities in ways that made them appeal to the consumer and how to mediate between the commodity and the consumer, for example, by distributing the commodities as personal gifts or by offering samples during presentations.

MLM and pyramid schemes used a unique form of personalized sales which allowed consumers to be targeted in intimate ways. As Carrier (1990) argues, a 'symbolism of possession' can be attached to commodities by the advertiser. Carrier shows how mail-order catalogues advertise objects as part of personal identities and social relationships, for example, by associating the commodities with the producer or by displaying the salespeople. A personal identity is being attached to the objects through which the appropriation of impersonal objects by the consumer may be encouraged. MLM companies also use catalogues, but the salesperson does not only appear in the catalogue, as in Carrier's example. He or she appears in person to present and discuss the catalogue, equipped with samples that can be touched, smelled or tasted. Some companies, such as Amway, organize meetings during which they demonstrate their washing powder and toothpaste and conduct little experiments that are designed to prove their supposedly miraculous effects. Moreover, the distributor is usually someone well known, a friend or an acquaintance, usually with the same ethnic and religious background. Distributors are instructed to be ready to advertise to anyone at any time, using personalized techniques such as telling potential buyers how they themselves have experienced the products or how they have helped their father, aunt or neighbour to become healthy and happy. The following quote is taken from an Amway guidebook for new distributors: 'Carry with you the oral spray Glister. When demonstrating it you can say: "This is an excellent product. I like to use it, it splendidly refreshes the breath. And this is so important during conversations."'

Companies teach their partners that they themselves have to become experts in the products or services they are selling in order to be able to advertise those commodities convincingly. What makes the schemes' sales practices different from other kinds of trading is that they present a story. Products or services are not simply offered to the customer, but it is explained in detail which ingredients cosmetic articles contain, which areas of health nutritional supplements are supposed to enhance or why people need health insurance. The logic of personalized sales allows the distributor to enhance the consumer's feeling that the products or services on offer are exactly what the individual client needs. Salespeople are schooled to take the perspective of the person to whom they want to sell something and to understand what this particular person might need in order to be able to advertise the product in a way that makes it interesting for the potential customer.

Such intimate confrontation with commodities stands in contrast not only to the more detached relationship between people and things in Soviet times that I have described above, but also to the ways in which commodities are usually offered in Aga today. Most small food shops, in particular, retain counter-service and sales clerks often appear less than eager to serve customers, let alone to make the shopping experience enjoyable for the buyer. The traders in the local market halls who compete more immediately make more of an effort to give advice to the customer or to find things in their shop the customer might want, but they usually have no detailed information about the ingredients, texture or quality of the predominantly Chinese commodities that they are selling. MLM provides a different kind of shopping experience and most of my informants said that they did not mind being offered commodities through distributors. On the contrary, many find it convenient to order and receive things through personal channels and find it an entertaining free-time activity to look at catalogues together. It is not the personal advertisement of commodities, but, rather, the aggressive attempts to recruit people into the companies that people perceive as problematic.

With the greater permeability of borders that followed the end of the Soviet Union, the new market was flooded with a large number of commodities that were either unbranded, falsifications of brand names or had brands with which people were unfamiliar (cf. Manning and Uplisashvili 2007). While the traders in Aga's markets sell an anonymous mass of consumer goods, MLM products are marketed as brands. Amway, Avon and Oriflame products, to name but a few examples, are well known and discussed in terms of their brand names. The companies strongly encourage and explicitly promote the idea that their products are superior to anything that can be purchased in the shops. Some distributors tell their acquaintances about the negative experiences they have had with articles purchased in shops; others show sections of TV broadcasts at their presentations that expose fake or flawed products being sold in shops. Thus, the distributors draw upon problems associated with an economy in transition in order to make their products appear as glorious exceptions. The narrative they construct and the explanations they provide sound plausible to people who live in a consumer environment in which a good deal of uncertainty is attached to new commodities.

Alisa, a woman in her mid thirties, joined Amway, but although she tried hard, she had no success marketing its products. At the time of our interview, she thought that the reason for her failure was that she simply had not invested enough time and energy into the project. Amway is a great company, she said, and its products are of high quality. For this reason, she continues to purchase them. When I asked her why she would not buy similar products in the town's drug stores for less money, she gave the following answer:

> I could, of course, but I'm not sure that they are genuine. There are many falsifications. You think it's Christian Dior which costs 1,000 roubles [around $15] here or 1,500 roubles there. But I'm not sure it really is Christian Dior, probably it's a fake. But regarding Amway I'm sure that it's genuine. There is a licence and so on … So in Amway you can afford genuine perfumes for 1,500 roubles. Perhaps they are not as well known as famous brands. But nevertheless they are probably safer, safer than [what can be bought] in the markets. There you buy something which makes you sick, it doesn't smell good or you can get an allergy. And [in Amway] everything is certified.

As her answer shows, Alisa associates the Amway brand with quality. She contrasts her trust in Amway products with comparable goods that she suspects to be fake. It is of course difficult to distinguish actual experience with products from commitment or loyalty to the company. This is true in particular because the companies encourage exactly the narrative used by Alisa. The distributors are likely to adopt the reasoning they learn in the companies even if it deviates from their own experience. One of my informants, Chimitma, an experienced distributor who has participated in many schemes, joined a new company called Faberlic during the time of my research. At one of our meetings, she showed me a catalogue of the company's products. She pointed out a washing powder to me that she praised as being of very good quality. When I asked her why she preferred this washing powder to the washing powders available in the shops, she gave a similar answer to Alisa. She said that washing powders from the shops were not good at all and that they would cause allergies. When I asked her whether she had experienced this herself, she answered that she had not, but this was what the company claimed. Unlike Chimitma and Alisa, people who had not been active distributors were sometimes more critical in their judgement of the quality of MLM brands. I will return to this point in the following section of this chapter.

The pyramid schemes use exactly the same strategies to advertise their goods and services as do the MLM companies. They use personal and intimate advertisements to convince people of their need for the goods or services offered along with the business opportunity. Here, I take a closer look at the services offered by the pyramid schemes and examine the particular ways in which they are related to the economic development that followed the collapse of socialism. The gap left by the retreat of the socialist state led to much uncertainty and, as will be shown, provided a fertile ground for frauds and scams of all sorts. Dubious companies, those running pyramid schemes amongst them, proliferated by occupying niches in the new market and were able to appeal to people seeking to protect themselves from the insecurities and threats facing them in a recently liberalized market environment.

One example of a market in which companies took advantage of widespread feelings of economic insecurity is in that of insurance. A plethora of companies offer private insurance services and, moreover, the possibility to earn money by selling insurance to other people. Turning clients into sales agents, they are operating according to a pyramid principle. Some of these insurance companies have turned out to be fraudulent pyramid schemes, such as a scheme called Global Trading Systems (GTS) that collapsed in 2011. GTS offered private pensions and health insurance that entitled people to free treatment in certain hospitals. Private health and age insurance are relatively new ideas for the people of rural Siberia, but are increasingly being recognized as a necessary substitute for the state services provided in Soviet times. Today, rural clinics provide insufficient medical treatment and many people receive pensions that lie only slightly above the subsistence level. People see a need for better healthcare and for private old-age provision. However, it is difficult to determine which insurance companies can be trusted and which are simply unstable and might go bankrupt. None of these companies has been in existence for very long and people have little experience in dealing with these matters. In the previous chapter, I introduced Zhalma, who had joined GTS and lost large sums of money when the pyramid collapsed. When I interviewed her, we also spoke about her initial motivation for joining GTS:

> Zhalma: They offered a private pension. I was convinced by the idea that I will have a private pension. And I invested my money.
>
> Leonie: You liked the idea of a private pension?
>
> Zhalma: I liked the idea, yes. They said I would have a private pension. And also voluntary health insurance. I was interested in these two things which the company GTS [offered]. But it collapsed, it doesn't exist anymore.
>
> Leonie: And these products, the pension and the health insurance, why did you think you would need them?
>
> Zhalma: I thought my pension will be small and it would be good to have a private pension as an additional pension. This is what I decided. Everyone needs voluntary health insurance. To get free treatment in clinics not only where you are registered but also in other parts of the region was tempting. Free treatment let's say in Chita or in Ulan-Ude or in Irkutsk.
>
> Leonie: And you don't have such insurance? I thought all citizens have health insurance.

> Zhalma: This is the obligatory health insurance. Everyone has it. But this was voluntary. We paid money every year in order to be entitled to treatment in these clinics.
>
> Leonie: And with this obligatory insurance you would not get the treatment? Why did you need additional insurance?
>
> Zhalma: They [the company] explained to us that this obligatory insurance is valid only at the place of registration. But the voluntary insurance is valid also in other regions. We can get treatment in Buryatia and in the Irkutsk Oblast and in Chita and here.
>
> Leonie: And why was it interesting for you to get treatment in other clinics?
>
> Zhalma: It was interesting because the doctors there are better than they are here. And I have health-related problems. Therefore I was interested and made this investment.

Again, it is unclear to what degree the appearance of the company actually determined the perception of the need for additional insurance. However, what we can see is that within the context of the emergence of new markets in a transitional economy, people like Zhalma, who have no experience of private insurance services and know little about how they work, are highly vulnerable to fraud.

A further example shows perhaps even more clearly how fraudulent schemes occupy new niches that appear within an unregulated market with insufficient consumer protection. I have described the enormous problem of household indebtedness and the desperate situation people find themselves in when having to pay most of their salaries and pensions to banks or loan sharks every month. The worst-case scenario is that people are unable to pay and, as a consequence, banks or collection agencies threaten to sue them. As a result, many people feel exploited by the banks and helpless in the face of their financial troubles. Increasingly, debtors simply stop paying their instalments, then living with the fear that their entire property might be confiscated.

Over the past several years, fraudulent schemes have appeared that offer to assist people in fighting the banks. They attract the interest of debtors by claiming that the banks broke the law by asking for exorbitant interest rates or by selling debts to collection agencies. Their lawyers can assist people, so they promise, in proving the banks wrong, thus relieving people of their debts. In addition to this service, for which participants pay significant fees each month, the schemes also offer the opportunity to earn money by inviting other people to join in order to be protected by their lawyers. Thus, the people who fall prey to these fraudulent schemes are those who are already in very problematic financial situations. The schemes promise the protection that the state fails to offer, with the consequence that the poorest and most vulnerable are doubly exploited.

The postsocialist market, then, offers fertile ground for the proliferation of MLM and pyramid schemes. The schemes not only appeal to people by offering a business opportunity in an environment where people see few other possibilities to make money, but also by occupying market niches with their goods and services and their intimate way of selling. The method of personalized advertisement mediates between the buyer and the product in novel ways, and narratives of quality appear attractive in a market environment in which counterfeit brand names are sold everywhere and many goods are of poor quality, resulting in a general uncertainty with regard to which goods and services can be trusted. However, as I will go on to show, interest in the products is often not the sole reason for their purchase and sometimes plays no part at all in the decision to buy. Rather, social dynamics play a crucial role in determining patterns of consumption, in particular in relation to MLM and pyramid schemes.

The Favour of Consumption

During my research in Aga, I discovered that distributors as well as nondistributors usually have several MLM branded products in their homes. When I spoke to people in their houses and our conversation turned to my research, they would frequently get up to look for a nutritional supplement, a tea or a cleaning product that they had either bought or received as a gift. One woman searched her cupboard for the tea that she could not find but was sure she had kept somewhere, while other informants searched for cleaning materials that they had purchased and explained that they never used them. One informant showed me a can containing a nutritional supplement and told me that there were boxes of them in his storeroom, but that his family did not like them. In short, MLM commodities were circulating that seemed to have little use-value for their owners. This, of course, raises the question why these people purchased the products in the first instance.

In order to answer this, we need to remind ourselves of the situation of many MLM distributors. In order to attain bonus levels within MLM companies that make their efforts worthwhile, distributors have to reach a certain sales volume. To achieve this sales volume, they can either purchase products themselves or sell them to others. Many distributors find themselves in a situation when they buy a stock of products the total sum of which guarantees them a bonus level and, only then, realize that they are unable to sell them. In this case, they can keep the products, give them away as gifts or hope that someone takes pity on them and buys the products despite having no real interest in them. My acquaintance Gerelma told me about one of her friends who had joined Amway and found herself in this situation. Her friend had placed a large order, but could not find customers for the toothpastes, boxes of washing powder and whiteners that were piling up in her home. Gerelma advised her friend to go to the villages to sell them, but despite all her efforts, her friend managed to sell only about a third of the products. Feeling sorry for her friend, Gerelma explained that she wanted to help and bought several of the items, although she neither wanted nor needed them.

I heard a similar story from a former Amway distributor who I interviewed. Damba, a middle-aged man who works as a vodka trader, told me how he had been persuaded to come to an Amway meeting and had been talked into signing a contract and buying the basic stock of goods. He tried selling the products, but found himself in the same situation as Gerelma's friend. At the time of our interview, he thought that if the market had not already been saturated, Amway could have worked for him. He also thought that if he had as many acquaintances as the Amway leader from Ulan-Ude, a well-known personality who invited him to join the company, it might have worked. But Damba could not sell what he had purchased, so he distributed everything among his relatives in the form of gifts. Although he lost money by joining Amway, the gifts he made will benefit him in the future, he said. His relatives would not forget the gifts and he was sure that they would support him by buying vodka from him in the future. Therefore, he reasoned, his investment was not a total waste of money.

In both these cases, products circulated despite the fact that consumers initially neither desired nor needed them. Gerelma bought products in order to help her friend who was in financial difficulties, whilst Damba's relatives received the products as unsolicited gifts. The latter example, in particular, shows how commodities may become embedded in local economic logics. Interestingly, Damba understood his gifts as part of an ongoing cultivation of relationships and a way to support his relatives. In turn, he expected that they would also support him – not necessarily by returning gifts, but within a commercialized market context. Here, once again, the entanglement between the capitalist economy and the gift or moral economy to which I have repeatedly drawn attention in previous chapters becomes visible.

Receiving commodities as gifts or doing someone a favour by purchasing them does not necessarily preclude interest in the object. One of my informants, Svetlana, explained that as a student, she used to buy Mary Kay cosmetics. She decided to try Mary Kay cosmetics because her roommate in Irkutsk worked as a Mary Kay distributor at that time and offered to place an order for her. Svetlana was curious about the products in the catalogue and she also wanted to support her roommate. She ordered a few things and liked them. After having finished her studies, she moved to Ulan-Ude. Now, she told me, she uses mainly Oriflame products. She explained that this is because she does not know a Mary Kay distributor in Ulan-Ude. Probably it would be easy to find one, she said, but she had not made the effort. In her opinion, the Oriflame products are as good as the Mary Kay products and her aunt in Ulan-Ude is selling them. Therefore, she now buys Oriflame cosmetic articles. Thus, by purchasing through MLM, Svetlana supports people she knows, but, at the same time, she does believe the products that she purchases from MLM companies to be of high quality. However, she is not interested in all the goods and services that are being offered to her. Her aunt is not only an Oriflame distributor but is also involved in several other companies, one of which is selling insurance. Whilst Svetlana is happy to buy cosmetics from her aunt, the insurance services do not interest her at all. Pressured by her aunt, she nevertheless bought the cheapest insurance available. 'How could I have said no? It's my aunt Soelma', she explained in justifying her decision.

As these examples show, the value of a commodity is not solely and sometimes not at all determined through the market within which it circulates. The fact that the commodities are being purchased does not reflect actual demand, and motivations are much more complex than most economic theories allow for. Purchasing a product through MLM or pyramid schemes does not necessarily mean that the product itself is seen as being valuable; rather, or additionally, it may mean that the relationship through which the product is purchased is seen as important and worth cultivating. The purchase may be an act of solidarity or the manifestation of a kinship obligation (cf. Sneath 2006).

The cultivation of the relationship lies not only in the act of purchase but also in the social event surrounding it. Looking at catalogues together with the distributor, discussing products, their prices and effects may be a leisure activity and a welcome interruption to everyday routines. Some companies, such as Tupperware, have made use of this opportunity and invented the famous Tupper-party (cf. Clarke 1999) or bingo games with Tupper prizes (de Vidas 2008).

The social event preceding the offer to purchase the products makes it problematic to reject it. Consumers report the difficulty of refusing to buy after distributors have invested efforts into coming to their houses, explaining and showing them products.

As I showed in detail in the previous chapter, the cultivation of relationships may be the reason not only for purchasing products, but also for participation in the schemes. Here, I emphasize that for many distributors, participation is not only a business but also a leisure activity. Their 'project' gives them a reason to get together and to meet new people from time to time. For *seteviki*, consumption is often tied to the relationships entwined with the goods. Seen from this perspective, the new communities of distributors and pyramid scheme investors become comparable to other subcultures that define themselves through shared consumer interests. As I have shown above, consumption may reinforce solidarities, but it can also create new solidarities within the corporate community. These new solidarities may reach far beyond the context of the schemes. During one of the Amway meetings that I attended in Aginskoe, this became particularly clear. One presenter was talking about Amway and what a great community the company offered. All its distributors, he said, would support each other. In the event that a partner falls ill and has to see a doctor, for example, this person could certainly jump the line in the hospital if the doctor was also an Amway member. This short account clearly reflects the logic of the local informal economy. It indicates the importance of personal solidarity in Aga's wider economy and shows MLM as embedded within it.

It is not only supply and demand, then, that determines the circulation of products sold through MLM and pyramid schemes. Social expectations and obligations steer consumer decisions as well as shaping corporate communities. As the examples given in this section have shown, monetarized market exchange cannot be separated from the framework of mutual support, particularly in Aga, where the latter has long been a defining feature of the local economy.

Magical Products

As I have emphasized from the beginning of this chapter, the primary consumers of MLM products are the people who market them. There is an evident logic to this phenomenon: if someone is sincerely interested in the product, this person is likely not only to purchase products, but also to register with the company. Registered distributors can consume at a reduced price and they have the option to also engage in the business of selling in which they might or might not be interested. Merely signing up for an MLM company is usually inexpensive and if the person intends to consume on a regular basis, it will be worth paying the fee. Furthermore, the distributor offering the products for sale will be more interested in registering someone than merely in selling them products, as this will save labour and potentially earn them bonus payments in the future. The boundary between the buyer and the seller is therefore blurred in MLM.

MLM and product-based pyramid scheme participants are encouraged to consume excessively for two main reasons. First, as discussed above, the MLM distributors need to achieve a certain sales turnover to reach bonus levels, thus making the business profitable for them. It is very difficult to find enough customers on a regular basis, and distributors often purchase considerable stock, which they have to use themselves if they cannot sell. The second reason is the focus of this section of the chapter: the companies teach their members that they have to become enthusiastic consumers of their production in order to be able to advertise it convincingly. For this purpose, a certain discourse is propagated that describes the products as unique and superior to all comparable products. Newcomers quickly learn to constantly praise the products they are selling, not only for the purpose of advertising it to potential customers, but also as a way of relating to others within the corporate community. They tell each other of the stunning effects of the cosmetic articles they have been using or the vitamins they have been drinking. As a response, they can expect compliments on their appearance or congratulations on their newfound health. Sponsors frequently ask their downlines about their consumption patterns and if it emerges that a distributor has not yet tried a particular product, they will be scolded for such failure. Thus, there is a constant internal control and pressure within the new community to consume.

Within this discourse, the products are attributed almost magical qualities. A washing powder is said to clean clothes without any effort; it is enough to dip them into the water and even the worst stains disappear immediately. Cosmetic articles are said to make people look young and beautiful, to solve all skin problems and make wrinkles disappear. With the help of the nutritional supplements and vitamins, consumers are said to acquire ideal weight and health. The partners learn to convince themselves of the power of the objects to bring about positive change in people's lives. Stories of the miraculous effects of the commodities are repeated over and over in informal discourse among *seteviki* as well as at presentations and seminars. The following example is an account about porridge, one of approximately ten products distributed by the pyramid scheme WIC Holding, which I introduced in previous chapters. It was narrated during a seminar for partners in August 2014:

> The second product of the third company TopQuality [part of the holding] is the unique 'Amaranth flip'. You all know what this 'flip' is, yes? Have you familiarized yourself with it? We have it on our homepage. You have probably read about the characteristics of amaranth? Our company is the first in the world to use amaranth seeds in our food products. What is amaranth? It is golden seeds which tolerate aridity. And in food products amaranth is used for the porridge of dry fruit jelly. Amaranth has a substance which is called squalene. Squalene removes heavy metals from the organism. It helps with oncology [*sic*!], it solves all problems. I use this product since last May. Why did I begin using this product? In 2010, when I was in Moscow at a conference, Dari-Suren from Ulan-Ude lived with me and she brought these cans with her. Back then I did not know about these products. I was buying only tea but she came with these cans. To my surprise she took out this [showing the can]. Fruit jelly, porridge, soups, all of these products. I said: 'Why do you carry all these cans to Moscow only for two or three days?' She said: 'This is my food, what did you think? I only eat these products.' And she told me her story. She had cancer, cancer of the fourth degree. Imagine her condition! She could not walk. Her husband had to carry her into her bed. She was almost invisible, so thin that she probably wore size 38 or something. When she was given the can she ate only fruit jelly. A teaspoon every day, every hour, even every second she ate this fruit jelly. Today she feels great. And the effect … when she went to the best hospital in Ulan-Ude after six months they were astonished: 'You are still alive?', she was asked by the doctors.

The account is a version of a typical narrative that I have come across in many of my conversations and interviews with people actively involved in MLM and pyramid schemes. The narrative idealizes the companies' products and praises them as powerful. The porridge is said to have unique, 'golden' ingredients and great healing power, sufficient to save a woman with cancer who medical experts believed to be incurably ill. The woman who told the story describes her puzzlement when she first witnessed consumption that seemed strange to her. But having acquainted herself with the products, she implies, she now understands why her acquaintance took the cans with her even on a trip to Moscow. Initial doubt with regard to the effects of the products is not unusual either, in particular when their use-value is questionable or when they are clearly overpriced. At first, people do not see why they should buy products such as nutritional supplements and the stories about the healing powers of vitamins or health pillows seem incredible or ridiculous to them. Often it is only with the decision to become actively involved that they begin to think of these items as important and indispensable. The process of becoming absorbed by the schemes, of becoming a *setevik,* is tied to a shift in perception of the value of the product. As the example above suggests, this is usually a shift from bewilderment to believing in the magical qualities of the products – in this case, porridge. I argue that such a shift in value is tied to the emotional relationship that the distributors develop with the objects and services they market.

As Foster (2005) argues, it is worth paying close attention to the ways in which a product becomes meaningful to consumers. The creation of value, from the consumer perspective, is absent from Marxist analyses of value that focus on production and is also absent from value chain analysis, most prominently theorized by Appadurai (1986). The latter tracks commodities in motion, studying shifts of value as things move through different contexts, but does not take into account historical and affective charges of objects. However, the creation of bonds between persons and things has been of vital interest to marketing experts. Foster draws on Kevin Roberts' argument that the advertising industry needs to 'tap into the biographical, sensual and emotional experiences of consumers' with the aim of establishing positive emotional responses to a product. Surplus value, Foster argues, is created through the consumer's work of appropriation, which consists in forming an emotional attachment to brands.

Miller (2001: 109) discusses how such attachment can develop even with regard to highly alienable commodities such as kitchen-cleaner or soup cans. In households, particular brands are sometimes used over several generations and represent not only tradition and stability but are also an expression of love and care among kin. Thus, the commodities come to resemble what Weiner (1992) describes as inalienable objects. In Miller's example, the relationship between consumer and commodity is shaped through a certain context in which the object comes to mean more for the person than its mere use-value. In the domestic context, which Miller describes, the commodity becomes associated with personal and emotional experience. A parallel can be drawn to the context of the schemes. As in Miller's case, the commodities are tied to a system of ideas and within this system they become meaningful to the *seteviki* on an emotional level. The goods or services are the basis for business and therefore for professional success. The brand comes to stand for everything the *seteviki* desire: for material wealth, travels to other countries and a career. In contrast to the domestic context described by Miller, it is not history and tradition that they are seen to incorporate, but future aspirations and desires. The products become symbols of hope.

However, there seems to be more to the attachment of distributors to the products they market than this symbolism. Distributors also become attached to the products they market in more immediate sensual ways. One almost gets the impression that the *seteviki* fall in love with the goods they are marketing. They speak about them with tenderness and affection, saying, for example, that they cannot live without them anymore. They use them constantly, carry them around as samples and speak about them to everyone they know. Moreover, they study them carefully in order to learn everything about them and experiment with their applications. As they become intimate with a commodity, it gains supreme value in their eyes and they cease to understand people who are not equally enthusiastic about the objects of their affection. A nutritional supplement, for example, transgresses its mere function of supplying the body with sufficient vitamins and comes to be perceived as a powerful medication for all sorts of illnesses. We could think about these commodities as part of an actor-network in the Latourian sense. Within a specific constellation of actors, the objects acquire significant agency and supreme value for those who advertise and consume them.

Conclusion

In this chapter, I discussed the role of the goods and services marketed through MLM and pyramid schemes. The fact that the MLM industry is somewhat estranged from its products because recruiting is more important than selling and the fact that in pyramid schemes, goods and services are secondary to their functioning do not mean that goods and services are insignificant in explaining the appeal of the schemes or the ways they function. I highlighted three socioeconomic spheres which define the relationship between people and commodities. First, I looked at MLM products and pyramid scheme services in the context of the postsocialist, rural market. I argued that the appeal of MLM products has to be understood in terms of their international branding and personalized advertisement, whilst in the case of pyramid schemes, their appeal lies in the particular niches they occupy within the liberalized economy. Moreover, I showed that the commodities come to appeal to people through the personal and intimate advertisement that characterizes MLM and pyramid schemes. However, it is important to note that it is not only, and perhaps not even predominantly, the market that determines the value of MLM and pyramid schemes products. The second context that I considered was that of the moral economy. In Aga, mutual economic support is of immense importance and purchasing products from someone is, under the current economic conditions, seen as a form of support. Buying from someone, as well as distributing commodities as gifts, can be part of the logic of long-term mutual support. As I have shown, the circulation of the products is embedded in social relationships and thus their purchase does not necessarily mean that they are seen to be valuable in terms of use-value; rather, the act of purchase may be valuable as a way of cultivating mutuality. Third, emotional and symbolic value can be attributed to the commodities. This is particularly salient within the microcosms of the schemes themselves. The *seteviki* develop intimate relationships with objects and services that assume such significance for them that it is hard to understand for those who are not involved. In conclusion, we can say that value can be attached to the objects in several ways: for some people, it is use-value; for many, the value consists in the cultivation of long-term economic and social relationships; and for the *seteviki*, the value of products certainly includes both symbolic and emotional dimensions. Therefore, the decision to purchase goods or services may not result from any interest in the commodities as such, but can express the hope of becoming a successful distributor, the desire to support a relative, the obligation to return a favour or the endeavour to become part of the community of *seteviki*.

6

Power in the Pyramids

The companies that operate MLM and pyramid schemes constitute very particular corporate forms because rather than employing a well-defined workforce, they invite a large and dispersed number of people to work for them. As detailed in Chapter 2, company managers have no legal obligation towards their workforce and they have very little control over them. This raises the crucial question of how they ensure that people act in their interest. This chapter is concerned with the mechanisms through which the workforce is disciplined and with the techniques through which the workforce disciplines themselves. More specifically, I am interested in how the distributors grow into their jobs, how they internalize corporate morality and why they are willing to keep working for companies even when they are not rewarded for their work or when there are clear indications of fraudulent activity.

Questions concerning the internal power relations of corporations have mostly been explored with regard to industrial work (e.g. Burawoy 1979; de Neve 2009; Nash 1979; Ong 1987). However, there is little literature on the ways in which power is exercised within modern business corporations or financial institutions. Ethnographies of the latter have instead focused on the employees' emotional experience of work (Zaloom 2006), the rationales that determine their decisions (Miyazaki 2003) or the moralities that guide them in their jobs (Appel 2014). An exception and, at the same time, an excellent example of the insights that an ethnography of institutional culture can provide on internal power mechanisms is Ho's (2009b) work on Wall Street investment bankers. By looking closely at the logics that steer investment banking, she explains how the system of short-term deal-based compensation works to encourage bankers to act in ways that are actually detrimental to themselves in the long run. As Ho's text shows, the anthropological study of institutional culture can reveal how corporate practices that are problematic for society as a whole can be legitimized within the institution itself.

Turning to corporate cultures in the MLM industry, Dolan and Johnstone-Louis (2011) have examined the discourses and practices aimed at producing disciplined Avon representatives in South Africa. The authors argue that the company encourages a process of self-disciplining in the Foucauldian sense. Like Ho, they contend that through certain 'calculative practices' such as incentives to earn a commission or encouraging the salesforce to dream of a better future, Avon aims to 'construct the subjectivity of the "empowered" entrepreneur' (2011: 27) from a distance. In this chapter I want to extend this discussion by showing that there are also more immediate ways of exercising power over the salesforce. I will show how pressure is exerted through the inner hierarchies of the companies and also how self-discipline is taught and learned. Rather than focusing entirely on the incentives companies offer, I argue that we have to take into account informal training as well as everyday interaction within the companies. The ethnographic examples I present here add to existing studies that look mainly at large-scale seminars (Cahn 2011; Jeffery 2001; Tereshina 2013; see also my examples in Chapter 3). While these accounts are important, they too easily generate the impression that people who join the companies are merely fascinated by dreams of riches and, as a consequence, try to make themselves into businesspeople individually and through their own strength of mind. As I will show in this chapter, the subjectivity of a distributor is not the product purely of individual effort, but of a network of social relationships. This chapter explores the mechanisms that tie people to the schemes and encourage them to act in the interests of the companies.

The first part of this chapter deals with the inner hierarchies of the companies. I will look at the relationships between people at different levels of the pyramid structure in order to see how information within the company gains authority. I will focus particularly on the ways in which newcomers learn about the company and grow into their role as businesspeople. This process will be explored in greater detail in the second part of the chapter, in which I discuss both the mental and the physical transformation of the self. In the third part, I will consider the ways that corporate logic in itself can be powerful. I will analyse the vicious circle in which adherents of MLM and pyramid schemes become caught and will relate it to an emotive structure that could be described as 'cruel optimism' (Berlant 2011).

Hierarchy and the Indoctrination of Economic Belief

The hierarchy among distributors and investors within the companies is reflected in their pyramid form. This pyramidal structure applies to MLM companies as much as to fraudulent pyramid schemes. Those at the top of the pyramid are more successful than those at the bottom because they profit from the investments or purchases of everyone they have recruited. While merit defines one's level in the hierarchy, the formal relation of all distributors/investors to the company is equal. Everyone has the same contract and, in theory, the same opportunities to build a large downline. There are no formally employed office managers, trainers or supervisors in Aginskoe, but these roles are filled by the distributors/investors on their own initiative. Authority, then, is largely informal.

Within the companies, hierarchy is celebrated. This is most visible at the seminars that I have described in Chapter 4. Those who have reached top bonus levels are given special roles at seminars. They are invited to share their stories of success and to explain marketing plans to a large audience. They occupy seats in the front row and are admired and treated as celebrities by all those who are less successful. But hierarchy is also enacted in less performative ways. It defines the interaction between *seteviki* on an everyday basis, in the offices, at local meetings and also privately.

Newcomers quickly learn that they need to subordinate themselves to their sponsor, the person who invited them into a scheme. In most cases, newcomers have a social relationship with their sponsor that precedes their entry into the company. The sponsor, having already offered guidance during the recruitment process, immediately becomes a mentor for the newly enrolled distributor/investor, providing introductory information and guidance regarding conduct to the newcomer. It is in the interests of the sponsor to take on this mentoring role, because they will only benefit from the newcomer if he or she works successfully.

Although, at the moment of entry, the sponsor is always higher up the pyramid, it is possible for newcomers to overtake their sponsors if they are more successful. This sometimes happens, for example, when the sponsor recruits only a single person and then gives up, but the newcomer continues working for the company and manages to recruit more than one person. However, in general, those who enrol first have the best chance of success because the market, over time, becomes increasingly saturated.

Newcomers are pushed hard by their sponsors to begin advertising the company and to recruit further people immediately, but in many cases, sponsors provide incorrect or incomplete information about the company, about the opportunities it offers or about the real costs linked to registration. Sometimes this is because they lack experience or knowledge, or have not fully understood the logic of the schemes themselves. But even those who know often keep quiet about the problems associated with their activity because if they told the whole story, their attempts at recruitment might well be compromised. Instead, they praise the schemes with as much enthusiasm as they can muster.

The sponsor is the most important contact person in the company for anyone involved in MLM or pyramid schemes. If questions or problems come up, so newcomers learn, they should ask their sponsor for advice. However, the sponsor is not the only person who has an interest in the success of the newcomer. The sponsor's sponsor and the whole upline can potentially profit from supporting the newcomer. Thus, corporate genealogy plays an important role and newcomers quickly learn about their uplines. They get to know them in the offices, at meetings or at business seminars in the cities. In the pyramid schemes I observed in Aga, senior operators connected with their downlines via Skype in order to motivate them or to give instructions.

In the following, I want to discuss two examples that demonstrate the significance of the companies' inner hierarchies and show how teaching and learning takes place along these hierarchies. The first example involves the Russian MLM company, NL International, which sells cosmetic articles and diet-related products. The second example refers to the pyramid scheme WIC Holding, which I have already discussed in some detail in previous chapters.

In October 2014, I participated in a meeting of NL International distributors in their office in the centre of Aginskoe. It was a small meeting. Apart from myself, only three people were present: Katia, the most successful local distributor who had introduced the scheme to Aga – she lives in Chita, where she learned about the company and was previously involved in several other MLM and pyramid schemes; Valeriia, a retired teacher who had been in the company for two years at that time; and Unerma, a meat vendor who had only recently joined NL International. All of them are Buryat women in their fifties to early sixties. Other distributors had been invited to the meeting, but had not shown up. When I arrived at the office, the three women were busy measuring their waists and discussing the NL International diet, which prescribes a strict use of NL International nutritional supplements. Soon, however, Katia said that it was time to start working. She began to explain the marketing plan, drawing numbers on a small whiteboard. She spoke about the large sums of money that could be earned, including bonus payments and percentages of the sales of others. Her account became increasingly complicated, and after five minutes I was no longer able to follow her confusing calculations. Katia herself got lost in the numbers and ended with the words 'to make it short, the money is spinning, it's spinning' (*koroche, den'gi krutiatsia, krutiatsia*). What she meant to demonstrate by means of her calculations was that the participants' efforts would certainly pay off. All of us had listened to the same story before. Valeriia had probably listened to it many times during her two years in the company and Unerma only a few times, since she was a newcomer. However, repetition is thought to be of the utmost importance in order to fully understand the information and to be able to pass it on to others. Katia then asked Valeriia to continue with a presentation of the company's goods. Reluctantly, Valeriia got up from her seat and excused her domestic dress. She told us about all the products that were exhibited on the small shelf in one corner of the office, praised the healing power of the vitamins, the effects of the nutritional supplements and the uniqueness of the tea. Where Katia found Valeriia's description insufficient, she corrected her and added further pieces of information. After finishing her presentation, Valeriia explained to me that she had learned to present the company's products, but that she could not yet present the marketing plan. Katia remarked that Valeriia still had to learn a lot, above all to open her mouth and to invite people into the company. Valeriia, obviously intimidated by Katia, looked down at the table with her head put in her hands and told us that she had tried to do so, but that she was simply not good enough. The day before, she had invited three people to come to the office, she said. Two of them had made excuses. The first woman said she would have to look after her children, while the second said that she had important things to do. The third person told her frankly that she knew that Valeriia wanted to sell her something, but that she did not want to buy it and simply walked away. Katia's response was that Valeriia needed to buy and use the products in order to convincingly market them to others. Valeriia responded that this time she was a 'bad girl' (*plokhaia devochka*) because she could not buy anything, but she promised to buy something another time.

Katia turned to Unerma, who had been scribbling notes during Katia's talk and now tried to please Katia with a short story. Recently, she had eaten in a cafe and afterwards had suffered a stomach ache. In the future, she would take NL International power bars with her and eat those instead of going to cafes. Katia, obviously content with the little story, suggested that Unerma should practise how to make phone calls. She asked her to immediately call her acquaintances in order to invite them to their office. Unerma, unhappy about this proposal, responded that she would prefer to call her acquaintances the next day. Katia insisted on at least practising a phone conversation in order to prevent the kind of mistakes that newcomers frequently make. She asked Unerma how she would start the phone conversation on the following day. 'I want to invite you to a certain place', Unerma said, uncomfortable with the whole situation. Katia, mimicking the role of her acquaintance, asked: 'Where do you invite me? Do you want to invite me to some marketing [company]?' Unerma did not know how to answer this question and Katia remarked triumphantly that she would now certainly understand that she still had a lot to learn.

The interaction between the three women clearly demonstrates the hierarchy among them. Katia is accepted as the boss of the office and as an authority who may command the other distributors. She is enjoying herself in the role of the instructor and exerts pressure on Valeriia, Unerma and others to consume the company's goods and to recruit further customers and salespeople. Katia pretends to have great knowledge regarding the company and conceives of herself as a professional. However, as her calculations demonstrate, she has only a limited understanding of the flows of money within the company. She exaggerates the possibilities it offers, but firmly believes that she is telling the truth. The other two women admire her conduct, her confidence and her success, which in her case is manifested in her rise to one of the lower bonus levels. Valeriia has less experience and is also less confident than Katia. She knows how NL International works and has registered a few people, but, unlike Katia, she does not perceive herself as a professional. Her comments reveal that she has a fairly precise conception of what professionality includes: an elegant appearance, full knowledge of the company and success in one's activity. Although Valeriia has already been registered as a distributor for two years, she continues to regard Katia as her teacher whom she would like to please. Unerma, who has recently joined the company, is only beginning to learn about it. Katia gives her advice and pushes her to take the next steps. What she has learned already is that certain narratives are expected of her, such as the narrative about the poor quality of non-NL International products.

Like NL International, the pyramid scheme WIC Holding organizes meetings of its investors for educational purposes. The WIC 'school' (*shkola*) combines two purposes: rather than being a one-way transfer of information from experienced teachers to non-experienced students, it is predominantly a training ground for partners with varying levels of experience. Unlike the business seminar discussed in Chapter 4, it is an internal event, not one of outreach. However, the procedures are little different from those of a seminar and contain the same elements: a presentation of the marketing plan, a presentation of the products and tales of success. Yet, in addition, it contains advice for participants – tips and tricks as to how best to conduct business. It is this internal advice that I now focus upon.

Fifteen people were present at the WIC schooling in Aginskoe in August 2014, all of whom were investors. As on other occasions when they gather, most of the participants had dressed up. The 'school' took place in the company's office and lasted for one complete day. Partners at various levels of experience took turns presenting blocks of information and in between speakers, videos made by the company were shown. One of these blocks concerned techniques of recruitment. Investors were advised that they should be well prepared for this task in order not to put off potential investors through clumsy recruitment attempts. The first step in the process, it was explained, would be to make lists of acquaintances. Investors should think of everyone to whom they are connected through social bonds, even if only distantly: old friends from school, their husband's colleagues, parents of their children's friends and so on. The second step would be to call these people. These calls should be aimed at getting people to come to the office and to listen to WIC Holding's business proposal. It was most important to make the calls with confidence and a positive attitude. If people were ashamed of what they were offering, the presenter explained, their project would be doomed to fail. The course of the phone conversation should be adapted to the social relationship with the person to whom one was extending the invitation. The audience was advised to see one of the company's leaflets for examples.

The following conversation is taken from the leaflet:

–Hello Olia!

–Hello Arkadii!

–Listen, I want to briefly tell you about something. We need to meet and talk.

> –What do you want to tell me about? You know that I have a family, children.
>
> –I see, and yesterday you didn't have children or what? I'm telling you, we have to meet.
>
> –All right, what do you want me to bring?
>
> –No, you don't understand me. It's not about drinking. I have to tell you something. Let's meet tomorrow night. And don't tell me that you have something else to do or that you have a headache or whatever. We will meet tomorrow at six o'clock. Take a pen and note down the address. I will dictate you the address, if you don't come I'll kill you.

An additional remark in the leaflet specifies: 'If you will say something like: "Please, my lady, would you be kind enough to grace us with your presence tomorrow" she will think that you have gone insane.'

If the phone conversation went well, the 'school's' audience was told, and a meeting at the office could be arranged, the partner should meet the guest outside the building. On the way to the office, guests should be told that they are about to meet a very important person, someone who earns a lot of money and who is very busy. Once in the office, the guest should be seated between the partner who has invited the guest and the partner's sponsor. As the more experienced of the two partners, it is usually the sponsor who provides the details about the company. The new partner should be present during the whole meeting in order to learn from their sponsor's explanations and to memorize information in order to later assist the partners he or she will recruit. Under no circumstances should the sponsor be interrupted or corrected because the sponsor is always right, the instruction continued. The most important aim during the first presentation of the company and the business plan to guests is to prevent them from leaving. Once guests realize that it is network business (*setevoi biznes*) they are being invited to, they need to be assured that the aim of the invitation is not to register them, but only to inform them properly. The partners should try to hold their attention by making clear how joining the company could benefit them and their family. Only during a second meeting should the marketing plan and the products be presented. For advice regarding the second meeting with the potential recruit, the *seteviki* connected via Skype to one of the company's well-known personalities who lives in Novosibirsk. When she appeared on the screen on one of the office's walls, everyone got up from their seats, greeted her and clapped. Then they listened to the woman's explanations for about 15 minutes, during which she detailed the order in which information about WIC Holding should be presented during the meeting in order to sound most convincing. When she finished, everyone clapped again and thanked her. More presentations followed, some of which were given by more experienced *seteviki*, while others were given by people who had been actively involved in the company's activities for only a few months. At the end of the day, the seven newcomers who were present at the event were asked to participate in the company's ritual of initiation. They had only recently joined WIC Holding and had not yet started practising to present the company at occasions like this. They had to get up from their chairs, introduce themselves and tell everyone about their aspirations. Then they were asked to symbolically part with poverty by smashing their cheap plastic pens on the floor. All of them followed the instructions, some reluctantly, others with confidence and enthusiasm. Finally, the newcomers were given new pens that were heavy and shiny. These pens, it was explained to them, were their tools for drawing marketing plans in the future and the first important step towards a professional performance.

These two examples provide glimpses of the circulation of information within the companies. The more experienced *seteviki* pass on their knowledge and ways of conducting themselves to less experienced distributors and investors. The inner hierarchy is important with regard to the authority of this information. Because newcomers learn to accept the more experienced participants, and in particular the sponsor, as teachers and to admire them as role models, the information received through them is rarely questioned. This is important to keep in mind if we want to understand why the information that trickles down from the top of the pyramid is powerful and readily accepted amongst those who identify with the companies. Furthermore, I observed that active participation was absolutely crucial for coming to believe in the viability of the economic model and in the promises of the companies. Newcomers are pushed to start recruiting immediately and by so doing, they begin to actively spread the information they have received. Recounting the narratives they have heard from their sponsor, repeating the promises to others and thus openly establishing themselves as representatives of the companies supports the appropriation of faith. Once more, it is worth drawing a parallel with evangelical Christianity. Simon Coleman (2003) argues that conversion is continuous rather than being confined to a momentary event. Proselytizing, he contends, is an important part of the conversionary process. Reaching out with the aim of converting others is a 'self-constitutive act' for his informants. 'Missionization is not merely a matter of attempting to transform the potential convert, but also – perhaps even primarily – a means of recreating or reconverting the charismatic self' (Coleman 2003: 17). The significance of proselytizing therefore lies not only in its outcome (that is, in whether it is successful or not), but also in the practice itself. At MLM and pyramid scheme seminars, be it large events or small-scale gatherings such as the examples discussed above, participants are preaching largely and sometimes exclusively to the already converted. The purpose of the events is only partly to recruit or to communicate new knowledge about the company. Attendees are usually familiar with most of the information conveyed at the seminars and they sit through repetitions of the same content over and over again. As my examples show, these events are also about practising professional performance, internalizing corporate philosophy and strengthening faith through collective rituals.

The examples I have given also show that the process of learning is tied to self-reflection. Valeriia and Unerma both started noticing habits or appearance that were not in line with the professional identities they were striving for. Valeriia obviously found it unproblematic to come to the meeting in her domestic dress, but as soon as she was asked to perform, she questioned her appearance. Unerma, who has certainly eaten in cafes many times in her life without reflecting on it, changed her opinion about food in cafes when she learned about the style of consumption encouraged by NL International (i.e. consuming only the company's products). The WIC Holding pen ritual encouraged exactly such a reflection upon one's identity and for some of the newcomers, it may have marked a symbolic parting with their previous ego. These moments of self-reflection are crucial in a process of personal transformation that is linked to becoming a *setevik* and they will be explored in more detail in the following section.

Transformation of the Self

> If five years ago someone would have told me that I close my wholesale warehouse and become a *setevik* I would have been seriously offended … But thank God I met my mentors. Firstly, they did not fit my image of a *setevik* and secondly, after our conversation I realized that for a long time I had just been stewing in my own juices … What I had been doing was all in the past and my income wasn't adequate. I understood this in my soul but couldn't accept it. After all I worked 15 years in the wholesale business.
>
> —Andrei Baikin, Magnitogorsk in an NL International leaflet

As I have already briefly discussed in Chapter 3, *seteviki* distinguish between their life before joining a scheme and their life after joining a scheme. This is an important part of the narrative they use when advertising their company, and I have encountered such narratives repeatedly within MLM and pyramid schemes. Within a few months, those who become actively involved experience a fundamental change in their identity, including their bodies, their attitudes, their dreams and their worldview (cf. Jeffery 2001). Most interestingly perhaps, they change their attitude towards the *setevoi biznes*, often radically, as the above quote demonstrates.

The process of the formation of the self was the focus of Foucault's later writing. Foucault understands subjectivity as historically constituted. Notably, he does not see the subject as a passive product of historical processes; rather, the subject constitutes itself actively through certain techniques that become available to them in their culture, society or social group. Thus, for Foucault, subjectivity is not static, but the ways in which we relate to ourselves and to our consciousness are dependent on historical conditions and may change over time (Kelly 2013: 512–17). Foucault terms the techniques and practices through which we constitute ourselves 'technologies of the self'. These technologies 'permit individuals to effect by their own means, or with the help of others, a certain number of operations on their own bodies and souls, thoughts, conduct, and way of being, so as to transform themselves in order to attain a certain state of happiness, purity, wisdom, perfection, or immortality' (Foucault 1994: 225).

Becoming a *setevik* is tied to hard work on the self, as many of my informants explained to me. As they are faced with constant rejection and even outright criticism, doubts in their own activity easily arise. In this section I provide glimpses of this struggle with the self in order to show how an established system of values has to be *actively* adjusted to conform to corporate logic and to the requirements of the job. This adjustment of ethics is tied to emotional hardships and a process of self-disciplining. Only if the newcomers manage to go through this process of personal mental transformation and if they start *believing* in the business project, as they describe it, do they have a chance of becoming successful.

One of my informants, Vadim, a man in his mid thirties who has worked for several MLM companies over the past five years, described to me in an interview how he went from initial rejection to the conviction that the business was worth joining. When invited into MLM for the first time by his acquaintance, Vadim was rather sceptical about the whole idea:

> Vadim: He picked me up, brought me to the office and familiarized me with this opportunity. Of course I didn't understand anything but, honestly, I felt uncomfortable rejecting his invitation and registered with Amway … I remember very well that when he presented [the company] to me for the first time he was inexperienced. It was obvious, he stammered, asked his mother something. Then, half a year later, I … I mean I registered and that was it, after that I didn't pick up the phone anymore when he called, I didn't pick up the phone because I didn't want to meet him anymore.
>
> Leonie: So actually, you didn't want to actively become involved?
>
> Vadim: Yes, I [registered] only, in order not to reject his invitation. Half a year later we met by chance, our acquaintance invited us to her home. I came with my wife and there was this guy. He presented [the company] again but this time clearly and professionally. His progress after half a year was visible. He had made progress and I thought: this is good. And then he began showing me his cheques. They were not big but at least they existed. So I thought: in half a year, nothing changed in my life and he is wearing a suit and is so respectable [*solidnyi*] and he was talking clearly and in an educated manner. And I asked him: 'Is my contract still valid?' 'Yes', he said. 'OK, let's meet again, you will teach me, I want to work actively.' At that time I had nothing in particular to do, I had a ton of free time but I needed some personal growth and so on.

Vadim started working for Amway. Soon, however, he realized how emotionally challenging the job was:

> In the beginning I was afraid of course. Like every beginner I was particularly afraid to make calls. I remember how the phone was shaking in my hand: 'There is this opportunity, let's meet!' On the other end of the line: 'Come on, which pyramid did you join?' You throw down the phone, you sit and think. There were moments when I almost gave up, I thought that I … I didn't believe, not at all, because I came up against so many refusals from relatives. They said: 'Go and find a normal job.' And from friends … But everyone I think experiences this, it is most important to get over this. And the reason why now half of my people don't work is that they came up against refusals. The most horrible thing is when you believe in and trust a person and you are torn over telling him about this opportunity.

Despite all his efforts, Vadim did not earn any money. He paid fees and bought products, but when he tried to sell them to his acquaintances, they said they did not need them. He was told by his sponsor that he would have to travel to a seminar in Moscow to learn how to professionally conduct business. Vadim bought a ticket and went to the seminar, all at his own expense. The seminar impressed him and he thought that he learned many new things there. Upon his return to

Aginskoe, he went about the business with renewed efforts. He read about the company, he studied the products, he went to meetings – again without success. He registered a few people, but they faced the same problems as he did and gave up their activity. Then Vadim's acquaintances told him about a different MLM company, Jeunesse, which sells cosmetic articles. Vadim decided to give up the effort to make money with Amway and instead began advertising Jeunesse. He thinks this business has better prospects than Amway because the market is not yet saturated. Moreover, Jeunesse works mainly with online invitations. This makes the job easier, he finds. Nevertheless, most people reject his attempts of recruitment. People would simply not believe in the opportunity, he explained. I asked Vadim whether he thought that MLM has changed his life. He replied:

> Yes. Not materially, of course. I don't drive a Mercedes and I don't go for a holiday every month but inside, inside. I now see that I used to be someone without aims, without dreams. I was like a blind kitten. I lived for the moment and didn't really aspire to anything. Here in Aginskoe, for example, I don't know about other places, in Aginskoe parents raise their children and teach them decency and honesty and when they grow up they raise their children. For them this is like the aim in life, to raise someone, to raise one's child. But this is not the main aim, I thought. It is important but I thought people should strive for something bigger, and it was MLM that gave me this world-view. I learned to dream, I learned to formulate aims, I now know why and what I aspire to. This personal growth and so on, all this MLM gives you. I perhaps changed inside but so far not outwardly. But I know that with this opportunity I will sooner or later change my life.

It was personal transformation that attracted Vadim to the job and it is what fascinates him about it, despite the fact that he does not earn significant amounts of money. He feels that he has gained a new perspective on the world and that he has learned to dream of a better future. What his account also reveals are the hardships that he has had to go through. It was the guidance of his sponsor, but also his desire to achieve what he thought worth achieving, that helped him to continue despite his experiences of failure and social rejection.

Inner conflict regarding values frequently surfaces among new distributors when they first join MLM or a pyramid scheme. Below I want to describe a situation I observed in the WIC Holding office on a late afternoon in August in 2014. Altana and Lubsama are both WIC Holding partners in their mid thirties. Altana joined the company in 2013 and has been working actively ever since. Lubsama registered in 2010, but she soon she gave up her activity. In the summer of 2014, she decided that she wanted to renew her efforts. She told me that she saw that some people had managed to become successful over the years and interpreted it as a good sign that the company still existed after four years. As a mother of small children, she was looking for extra income with a flexible work schedule and thought it would be worth trying again. One afternoon, I was sitting in the office with the two women, who were both working. Lubsama had convinced an acquaintance whom she had met by coincidence in the street to come to the office. The elderly woman did not know why Lubsama had brought her to the office. As soon as she understood where she had been invited, she got up and left, saying that she had heard about this sort of opportunity many times and that she knew that it would be necessary to invest money. Lubsama then made a phone call, inviting someone to a second meeting. I could tell by her answers that she received a negative response to her invitation and was asked why she got involved in this kind of business. 'What other options do I have? I don't want to work for 12,000 roubles [around $180] a month', she said. After finishing the call, Lubsama confessed to Altana that she found people's reactions quite disheartening. She said that she was considering calling another woman, but was hesitant because she knew this woman to have had negative experiences in MLM. The woman had bought products and then had been unable to sell them. Altana advised Lubsama to definitely call and invite her, as the woman had most likely made a mistake or had been ill-informed. It would certainly be a great opportunity for her to join WIC Holding.

The case is interesting because it shows that Lubsama had made the decision to become an active partner, but she had not yet fully adopted the mindset that would help her to overcome doubt. In contrast to many *seteviki* I met, she was still able to see her own decision, as well as the position of others, within larger social contexts. Her reaction on the phone is one indication. She did not explain her decision to join the company by elaborating on the advantages the company offers and the good it does in the world, which, according to corporate instructions, would have been the 'correct' answer. Instead, she expressed her perception that she lacked alternatives. Furthermore, Lubsama is not yet convinced that the scheme offers a great opportunity for everyone. She does not feel comfortable inviting her acquaintance who had already lost money in similar schemes. It is an ethical problem that prevents her from pushing forward the company's and her own interests. Altana, a more experienced *setevik* and superior in the hierarchy, knows the 'correct' justification: failure has to be attributed not to the system or to personality, but simply to insufficient knowledge or incorrect practice. Lubsama learned from Altana how to frame the problem within the company's logic, which might help her to conduct business in the future or, if she does not find it convincing, will most likely lead to her giving up her activity fairly quickly.

Becoming a *setevik* is associated with a transformation of the self. This transformation includes adopting an appearance and learning a form of conduct that is associated with professionalism, but also includes a less visible, inner transformation. As I have argued, this transformation is linked to a shift in the personal value system. As Vadim's account exemplifies, *seteviki* often assume a critical distance from their life, or the lives of people around them, before entry into the scheme. Joining a scheme requires embracing a new belief system. This includes learning to dream and to aspire to new goals, but it also includes overcoming doubts and adjusting to corporate ethics and corporate reasoning. As demonstrated in both Vadim's and Lubsama's cases, this is emotionally challenging because the belief system is not shared by the wider society. The process of personal transformation includes an active shaping of subjectivity in Foucault's sense (cf. Dolan and Johnstone Louis 2011), but it is assisted by the companies through the cultivation of inner hierarchies and through teaching and learning in ritualized ways. Internalized power certainly plays an important role in the schemes and it is worth bearing in mind that the idea of making oneself into a businessman or a businesswoman reflects a broader neoliberal discourse in Russia (cf. Yurchak 2003). We should not, however, lose sight of the role of the companies as powerful agents and corporate logic as driving force behind the decisions people make.

Victims or Perpetrators?

Above, I have discussed how newcomers learn about the companies, how they are trained in their jobs and how, under the guidance of more experienced *seteviki*, they undergo a process of personal transformation towards a physical and mental state that is necessary in order to successfully conduct business. This process is ongoing and even professional *seteviki* think that they can always improve their performance. As soon as newcomers start working actively, they become representatives of the company, even though they may know very little about it and often have no clear idea of the consequences of their activity. I have argued that active proselytizing is important for appropriating and reinforcing belief in the systems of MLM or pyramid schemes. Consequently, the active advertisement of the schemes means that it becomes increasingly difficult to acknowledge flaws in the system or to accept indications of fraud. I now move to show how *seteviki* become caught in the belief system by its internal logics.

Lauren Berlant has described the condition of people who are trapped in their fantasies of the 'good life' and cling on to something that is actually an obstacle to their wellbeing as 'cruel optimism':

> Whatever the *experience* of optimism is in particular, then, the *affective structure* of an optimistic attachment involves a sustaining inclination to return to the scene of fantasy that enables you to expect that *this* time, nearness to *this* thing will help you or a world to become different in just the right way. But, again, optimism is cruel when the object/scene that ignites a sense of possibility actually makes it impossible to attain the expansive transformation for which a person or a people risks striving; and, doubly, it is cruel insofar as the very pleasures of being inside a relation have become sustaining regardless of the content of the relation, such that a person or a world finds itself bound to a situation of profound threat that is, at the same time, profoundly confirming. (Berlant 2011: 2, emphasis in original)

Berlant reminds us that sentiments that project the future in a positive light may actually be quite destructive in their effect. Caught in fantasy, we might be trapped in practices that lead away from what we are longing for. That we do so is not irrational or erroneous, because we may find comfort within these emotions. Optimism is 'a scene of negotiated sustenance that makes life bearable as it presents itself ambivalently, unevenly, incoherently' (Berlant 2011: 14).

During my research, I met several *seteviki* who had lost their reputation as well as their money in MLM and pyramid schemes, but nevertheless kept getting involved in new schemes. These *seteviki* were those who defended the positive nature of the schemes with the greatest vehemence. They were convinced that it was not the pyramid structure of the schemes that was problematic, but their own lack of ability, training or enthusiasm. I suggest that it is helpful to imagine these people as caught in a state of 'cruel optimism'. As we have seen in Vadim's case, he continued working for Amway even though he did not make any money. And despite the fact that he experienced how difficult recruitment was for himself, he kept inviting others into the scheme. Even after several years of involvement in various companies, he firmly believed that one day his efforts would pay off. By maintaining their attachment to the fantasy of the good life, many *seteviki* are drawn deeper into debt along with the people they encourage to register and thus counteract their own material interest while finding comfort in their vision. The theoretical framework of 'cruel optimism' can contribute to an understanding of why people stick to a practice despite all indications from their own experience that it will not bring them closer to their hoped-for goals.

In the following, I want to give two examples that show that this optimism can be strong enough to explain away even clear indications of financial fraud in the case of pyramid schemes.

At one of the WIC Holding 'schools' for partners that took place in October 2014, Dashima, one of the locally most active *seteviki*, reported on her journey to Cyprus, where the company's main seminar had taken place a few days earlier. A group of five partners from Aginskoe who had been able to afford the air fare had participated in this seminar, at which the company's charismatic founder, Arkadii Sharov, performed. Sharov had good news for them, Dashima explained. WIC Holding was about to expand into the Chinese market – a great opportunity for all its partners because of the millions of potential new recruits. A limited number of 'China shares' would soon be offered to the partners and Sharov recommended buying these shares at the first opportunity. But there was other good news: WIC Holding had set itself the new goal of becoming a monopolist of MLM. According to Sharov, this aim would be achievable because the company already had the most talented workforce of all MLM companies.

Having finished her account of the good news, Dashima turned to the not-so-good news. Just like good news, she said, these would be part of every business and the company should be credited for openly communicating this to its partners. The nightclub on Cyprus for which almost everyone present had bought one or more shares had not yet been built. This was the explanation for the (at that time already five-month) delay of the expected payout for which the investors were anxiously waiting. At the seminar in Cyprus, they had been told that the reason for the problem was another company that was responsible for the building project. But there was no need to worry, Dashima assured the participants. WIC Holding had already made plans to build another nightclub, one with large dance floors and awesome light effects where all sorts of events would take place in the future. This nightclub would be even better than the one that had been planned originally and therefore it would attract more people. Thus, the value of the shares would increase and the payout would be even higher than anticipated. From previous conversations with the partners, I knew that they were desperately waiting for the promised returns on their money and I was therefore surprised that none of them complained when they heard the news and that no questions were raised. Instead, Dashima moved on to the next topic.

The company was excused by Dashima and others, despite its obviously false promises and despite the fact that they themselves were amongst its victims. But what choice did they have? If they admitted that they had become the victims of a scam, they would have had to give up their vision, accept the loss of what is, to them, a great sum of money and, perhaps even more problematic psychologically, admit that they had been accomplices in illegitimate economic activities, as they themselves had drawn people into the scheme.

In such cases, as the following example shows, *seteviki* may even blame themselves for misunderstanding in cases in which the companies do not deliver what they have promised. The company iWowWe is a pyramid scheme that markets communication software similar to Skype. In 2012, iWowWe representatives promised people in Aga free internet access if they joined the company. This promise was highly effective in making the product attractive in Aga because, at that time, few households were connected to the internet. However, as it turned out, people who joined the company were not given free internet access. Zhalma, one of the investors, remembers that at first they all thought that they would get free internet access. But this, as she put it, was only what they *thought* the company had promised; it was not what the company had *actually* promised. Obviously they had misunderstood those further up in the pyramid because they had little understanding of these things ('my zhe ne gramotnye' – 'we have no financial literacy'). In retrospect, Zhalma and others who are currently working for the company created an explanation for the unfulfilled promise that put the blame on themselves rather than on those higher up in the pyramid, including its founder. Attributing the false information to their own ignorance, they were able to protect their view of the company's integrity, which was essential to keeping their project going locally.

Both cases reveal strategies through which active participants defend the legitimacy of their scheme, although they are confronted with what, to an outsider, appear to be obvious indications that they have become victims of fraud. In the WIC Holding case, the solution was to accept the explanation provided by the founder of the pyramid scheme that refers to factors external to the scheme and shifts responsibility, while in the second case, the problem was blamed on their own misunderstanding of the situation. I have encountered both strategies frequently in both MLM and pyramid schemes in cases in which things go wrong, whether because the expected money does not arrive or if, despite all efforts, no money can be earned. Seen from the perspective of *seteviki* who have recruited other people into the schemes, such rationalizations make sense. On the one hand, as argued above, they are caught in an emotive structure that could be described as 'cruel optimism'. If they question the company, they undermine their own authority as its representatives and, consequently, the loss of their job, their investments and their vision would logically follow. But what might be even more difficult to deal with is responsibility in such a case. As *setevik*, one has attracted others into the schemes, perhaps unaware or only half-aware of the consequences of one's activity. By acknowledging that the company has failed to fulfil what it promised, *seteviki* would be admitting that they themselves made false promises to people to whom they are connected by close social ties. Acknowledgement of fraud would mean acknowledgement that they themselves had actively increased the number of victims of the schemes. It is for these reasons, I suggest, that once someone has managed to overcome initial doubts and has started recruiting systematically, in particular in pyramid schemes where high sums of money are at stake, it is psychologically very difficult to give up that way of thinking and acting, whatever the evidence with which one is presented.

Here we are dealing with a form of power that is inherent in the corporate structure of MLM and pyramid schemes. In addition to direct pressure and the exertion of power over the self, the logic of the schemes keeps people attached to the companies. It is the complicity arising from the active proclamation of the companies' trustworthiness that blurs the boundary between victims and perpetrators.

Conclusion

In this chapter, I discussed the corporate culture of MLM and pyramid schemes with a focus on internal power dynamics. Whereas in previous chapters, I looked at ways in which the companies exert power externally in order to gather recruits, here I was interested in the various forms of power that bind recruits to the schemes in the long term. I argued that it is not merely incentives such as the promise of wealth or bonus payments that motivate *seteviki* and make them act in the interests of the company; it is the corporate organization of local communities of *seteviki* that has a crucial impact on the formation of entrepreneurial identities. Through informal hierarchies, information is distributed within the schemes and direct pressure is exerted from the top down. The local group, which represents the company, also assists the individual process of professional and ethical self-formation.

The experience of psychological strain can be shared and ritualistic affirmation of the companies' greatness is effective in scattering doubts. Finally, corporate logic pushes participants into responsibility they might become aware of only when it is too late. Caught in the emotional trap of 'cruel optimism', they keep pushing forward what they cannot undo and collectively create justifications for their activity, along with explanations for failure.

Conclusion

This study of MLM and pyramid schemes in a Siberian town has focused on the question of how popular and speculative capitalism appeals to people and how the illusion of future wealth attracts investors and believers. As an anthropologist, I was, of course, interested in exploring the local manifestation of the schemes. I have shown how MLM and pyramid schemes are embedded in the postsocialist economy and how new economic practices and ideas overlap with culturally specific economic patterns and ideals.

One of the key aims of this book was to provide a picture of how people in Aga experience capitalism, how they understand capitalism and what hopes they have with regard to the capitalist future. I have studied these questions in a newly capitalist environment and with regard to one of capitalism's most radical and blatant appearances that I think was suited to make clear to the reader the economic situation and the economic prospects of the local people in the global capitalist economy.

While looking at the local manifestation of the schemes in Siberia, I have also repeatedly emphasized the globality of MLM and pyramid schemes. I have shown how MLM developed in the United States and how, based on key ideas of the American dream such as equal opportunity, the ethic of hard work and the ideal of the self-made man, the industry spread around the world. Pyramid schemes are likewise proliferating worldwide and I have demonstrated how similar they are to MLM in their structure and their promises.

A close look at the schemes can provide unique insights into their social dynamics and is useful for understanding their popularity as well as the problems inherent in them. However, it is also important to see MLM and pyramid schemes in larger economic contexts and in relation to worldwide economic trends. I therefore want to conclude this book by zooming out of Aga in order to compare the schemes to similar economic phenomena and see them in the context of broader economic developments.

From the beginning, I have distanced myself from the agenda of the schemes and have taken a very critical stance. I think that the social pressure within MLM and pyramid schemes, the unfulfilled hopes associated with them and the problematic financial consequences for the majority of participants have become apparent in my ethnography. However, rather than discarding MLM and pyramid schemes as curiosities, eccentricities or manias, I think that they can teach us something about the challenges we face in our capitalist world today.

Multilevel Marketing and the Gig Economy

In recent years, the phrase 'gig economy' has increasingly come into use. The gig economy describes a labour market that is characterized by part-time, short-term or freelance work arrangements as opposed to permanent jobs. Workers get paid for the 'gigs' they do – for example, a car journey or a food delivery – but they do not get a regular wage.

The fact that more and more people find themselves in such work arrangements is assessed differently: proponents celebrate the gig economy as providing greater flexibility with regard to employment hours and therefore guaranteeing freedom and independence for the workers, while opponents see the gig economy as a form of exploitation. The clear advantage for the employers is that they only pay when work is available and have no staff costs when there is no demand. Workers have the status of independent contractors, which means no minimum wage, no paid holiday, no sickness pay and very little workplace protection.

Companies like Uber, which offers the technology for peer-to-peer transportation service, or Deliveroo, a food delivery company, have received a lot of media attention lately because they have become the subject of protest and legal action. At the heart of the controversy surrounding the gig economy lies the issue of workers' rights. Uber and Deliveroo are prominent examples, but are far from the only companies that hire workers as independent contractors. They stand for a much larger trend towards precarious working conditions that benefit the companies while putting a lot of people, who mostly 'gig' out of necessity, in difficult situations.

Interestingly, Amway and other MLM companies have recently begun to describe themselves as part of the gig economy. Jim Ayres, the Managing Director of Amway North America, for example, compares direct selling to ride-sharing and home-sharing, and writes about the advantages he sees in the gig economy:

> These kinds of opportunities are so appealing mainly because they provide benefits not often found in 9-to-5s – there are minimal barriers to entry, an inherently low financial risk, and flexibility in regards to time commitment and schedule. Almost all 'gigs' are similar in the fact that they don't require a certain degree, have very little, if any, upfront costs and allow participants to set their own hours – oftentimes around a primary job and family obligations. (Ayres 2016)

John Parker, Amway's Chief Sales Officer, envisages direct selling as a prospective business opportunity because, as he puts it, people are increasingly attracted by flexible work arrangements:

> I think today the opportunity for direct selling is better than it has ever been. We know from the Amway Global Entrepreneurship Report that over 75 percent of people in the world are positive towards entrepreneurship. In addition to that we have seen an environment where the gig economy and the desire for flexibility that people have and how they work, whether it is as independent contractors or owning and operating their own small businesses is very appealing.[1]

From the perspective of Amway representatives and other proponents of the gig economy, people choose to be part of the gig economy because they value flexibility or dream of being independent. Uber, for instance, advertises its job opportunity as: 'So you're thinking about driving with Uber. You like the idea of choosing your own hours, being your own boss, and making great money with your car.' Since income is entirely based on merit, there is no income security for Uber drivers or Amway distributors. If workers are not adequately compensated for their working hours, the companies attribute this to their laziness or accuse them of working inefficiently.

Just like MLM, Uber and other companies working with independent contractors are controversial enterprises and are frequently subjected to lawsuits. Uber, to stick to my example, agreed to pay $20 million to settle claims by the U.S. government that it was misleading drivers with regard to prospective earnings. According to the Federal Trade Commission, Uber had exaggerated the income opportunities while downplaying the costs of renting or hiring a car (Bartz 2017). This is strongly reminiscent of the allegations raised against Amway with regard to the money people could make as distributors, which I have detailed in Chapter 2.[2]

The gig economy casts work as an assemblage of opportunities. At its basis lies a radical market ideology. The market regulates the price paid for the work, everyone is responsible for themselves and their choices, and companies have little if no responsibilities vis-à-vis their workforce. Proponents, of course, forget to mention those who suffer from such working arrangements and their consequences, those who have no other option than to accept the opportunities defined by the companies and are therefore vulnerable to exploitation, and those who try their best before realizing that it is not to their benefit because they have been misinformed.

Amway and other MLM companies can be seen as early examples of the gig economy. However, there is a particularity about the industry that sets direct selling apart from other gigs: its missionary agenda and the fact that the recruitment of further workers, who will sell products to the benefit of those who have recruited them, makes MLM potentially very profitable. This introduces a speculative dimension to the industry. MLM is more than selling something here or there in order to make some extra money. The idea of building downlines by recruiting further distributors and by profiting from their work opens up a space of imagination – the imagination of wealth.

The forms of exploitation we find in MLM are similar to those of the gig economy more generally. However, in addition to that, MLM is based on a form of exploitation that we could describe as emotional. MLM relies on people's hope. It is because of the vision of a better future, which the industry successfully evokes in many people, that working conditions are accepted.

There is an important literature on the role of emotions in capitalism, exploring forms of emotional labour (Hochschild 2012) or ways in which intimacy is created and negotiated through economic activity (Zelizer 2005). It is demonstrated how economic relations can be deeply emotional, while intimate relationships may be defined by economic rules (Illouz 2007). Departing from these ideas, I think it would be worth thinking more about how companies manage to encourage certain emotive structures in order to make their workforce bear difficult working conditions.

We can observe these emotive structures not only in corporate environments but also, for example, in the academic sphere or in the media sector. Academics and journalists have to accept short-term contracts or freelance work, they have to be highly flexible with regard to where they work and have to be on a constant lookout for the next opportunity. Working under such conditions is not celebrated as freedom, but it is widely seen as structural problem posed by neoliberal trends. Often it is the hope to eventually manage to secure one of the rare positions that offer security that is crucial for the motivation to continue working in these spheres.

More systematic research into the ways in which people perceive of their work, what they value about their work and, perhaps most importantly, how they feel about their work is needed. These insights are necessary in order to counter the logic of those who claim that people enjoy precarious working conditions because they want to be flexible and independent. This is a dangerous neoliberal discourse that mainly benefits those at the top of the pyramid and contributes to deepening already-existing economic inequalities.

Pyramid Schemes and Finance Capitalism

Since the 1970s, we have witnessed a considerable loosening of regulatory constraints in the field of finance. This allowed for the emergence of new financial markets and different kinds of futures trading. The new significance of finance meant a power shift away from production. It is no longer increases in manufacturing capacity that account for rising per-capita incomes, but financial services that secure the wealth of a nation. Therefore, the integrity of the financial system has become a key concern for neoliberal states (Harvey 2005).

As I have discussed in the Introduction to this book, it is important to consider the consequences of these developments in places far from financial centres. In today's globalized economy, flows of capital and turbulences in financial markets affect people even in remote and rural places. Edward LiPuma and Benjamin Lee have described the effects of speculative finance on the economic periphery as a new form of violence and, more specifically, as 'abstract symbolic violence' (2004: 26). The violence is symbolic because it is not exerted by military force or colonialism and it is abstract because it hides behind local realities such as food prices, interest rates or declining social welfare programmes. The global financial system affects local communities who have neither insight into its mechanisms nor control over its effects.

I have described the effects that neoliberal state building had in Russia. I have drawn attention to the consequences of financialization, in particular the privatization of the banking system, and I have discussed what the proliferation of consumer loans with exorbitant rates of interest meant for the population.

Again, while some see finance capitalism as a blessing and celebrate the incorporation of poor populations into the banking system or see the access to microcredit as a great opportunity, others point to problems such as rising social inequality, household indebtedness and new forms of social conflicts emerging from this. People around the world are confronted with the effects of neoliberal policies, and pyramid schemes can be seen as an answer to that. Participation is linked to the attempt of understanding opaque financial logics and the desire to also get a piece of the speculative cake.

Instead of protesting against the conditions they are suffering from, my informants were trying to develop individual solutions. Abstract symbolic violence is hard to get at, of course. The financial system and the neoliberal forces behind it are not recognized to be the problem by local people. Trying to profit from the system, on the other hand, is tempting and MLM as well as pyramid schemes offer themselves as instruments to do so. Rather than seeing themselves as oppressed workers, people prefer to imagine themselves as competitive protagonists of capitalist growth. This is not only true for MLM participants, but it is also a more general trend that points to a global crisis of the kind of political thinking that debunks economic oppression.

MLM and pyramid schemes, as I have shown throughout this book, offer agency. They do not merely provide a system of belief, but they tell people exactly what they need to do in order to profit from it. They offer a plan of action that gives hope. Moreover, they offer a reasoning that lets exploitative structures and financial scams appear as systems that can benefit everyone. They use the same arguments as the proponents of the gig economy and the same arguments of those advocating aggressive neoliberal strategies. It is, I think, worth spending the last lines of this book on a brief thought experiment that sees the schemes not only as a radical form of capitalism but also as a reflection its logic.

Mirrors of the Capitalist System

MLM and pyramid schemes, I suggest, exemplify a crucial systemic logic of capitalism and reflect some of the problems associated with it.

First, there is the axiom of growth. The schemes cultivate the illusion that their growth is indefinite. This illusion is necessary to sustain the idea that all participants can profit from the schemes. In fact, growth is limited. This means that anyone can be successful, but not everyone will be successful. Therefore, in order to fuel the proliferation of the schemes, and capitalism more generally, the idea that growth is limited has to be concealed. The belief in the system needs to be strengthened by the rhetoric of possibility, which encourages attempts to become successful. This is crucial because all attempts that are made to become successful sustain the system.

Second, there is the issue of inequality. Since growth is limited, the systemic logic of MLM and pyramid schemes generates winners and losers. While winners are few in number, there are plenty of losers. They have worked for the system hoping that they would eventually become one of its winners, but they have failed. Perhaps they did not belong to the fastest, hardest-working individuals or perhaps they did not belong to those who managed to market themselves, the products or the purported opportunities aggressively enough. Perhaps it is those people who recognized the problems inherent in the system and refrained from taking it further. Certainly, however, they were not rewarded adequately for sustaining the system, and guaranteeing MLM companies and their successful representatives their profits.

Third, there is the narrative of possibility. According to the logic of the American Dream, one can achieve anything if one only works hard enough. However, in order for this to be true, one needs to be lucky: one needs to be healthy, one needs to be flexible and one needs to be in the right place at the right time. Moreover, one needs to embrace and believe in the logic that working hard in order to triumph over others is a desirable aim in life. Possibility is celebrated in MLM and pyramid schemes, while probability is dismissed. The vision of the individual's future is the driving motivation behind the work one is doing, while the hardships of the present are endured because of the hope they provide. Considering the likelihood of whether one's efforts will be rewarded adequately is taboo because it would, of course, harm the dream.

MLM and pyramid schemes are systems that enable 'accumulation by dispossession' (Harvey 2005). They commodify social relations in order to channel money towards the top of the pyramid. They rely on spatial expansion because markets quickly become saturated and new resources – i.e. new recruits and their relations – are needed.

A look behind the scenes of MLM and pyramid schemes clearly shows the shadow sides of certain capitalist promises and logics. The fact that MLM is classified as a legal activity whereas pyramid schemes are regarded as a scam is telling, especially considering that my ethnography shows how similar these practices really are. If legitimate and illegitimate economic activity cannot be neatly separated from each other, then this should make us suspicious at least.

Notes

1. Retrieved 18 November 2018 from https://www.youtube.com/watch?v=GOhC_hGoUHg.

2. For a well-researched comparison between Amway and Uber, see the article by Petey Menz, Did Amway Create the Gig Economy?' Retrieved 18 November 2018 from https://www.theawl.com/2017/07/did-amway-create-the-gig-economy.

References

Albaum, G., and R.A. Peterson. 2011. 'Multilevel (Network) Marketing: An Objective View', *Marketing Review* 11(4): 47–361.

Amway. 2018. 'History Timeline'. Retrieved 20 November 2018 from http://www.amway.com/about-amway/our-company/heritage/history-timeline.

Anderson, D. 2000. 'Surrogate Currencies and the "Wild Market" in Central Siberia', in P. Seabright (ed.), *The Vanishing Rouble: Barter Networks and Non-monetary Transactions in Post-Soviet Societies*. Cambridge: Cambridge University Press, pp. 318–44.

Andrews, E. 1997. 'Behind the Scams: Desperate People, Easily Duped', *New York Times*, 29 January. Retrieved 4 December from http://www.nytimes.com/1997/01/29/world/behind-the-scams-desperate-people-easily-duped.html.

Appadurai, A. 1986. *The Social Life of Things: Commodities in Cultural Perspective*. Cambridge: Cambridge University Press.

Appadurai, A. 2012. 'The Spirit of Calculation', *Cambridge Journal of Anthropology* 30(1): 3–17.

———. 2013. *The Future as Cultural Fact: Essays on the Global Condition*. London: Verso.

Appel, H. 2014. 'Occupy Wall Street and the Economic Imagination', *Cultural Anthropology* 29(4): 602–25.

Ayres, J. 2016. 'Not All Gig Economy Opportunities are Created Equal'. Retrieved 20 November 2018 from http://www.amway.com/en/Documents/AMWAY-US-Business-Executive.pdf.

Baikal-media. 2005. 'Zaiavlenie Alekseia Krasnopeeva Po Povodu Skandala Vokrug GTS Union'. Retrieved 1 September 2018 from http://www.baikal-media.ru/news/conflicts/22124.

Bakan, J. 2005. *The Corporation: The Pathological Pursuit of Profit and Power*. London: Constable.

Bartz, D. 2017. 'Uber to Pay $20 Million to Settle U.S. Claims It Misled Drivers'. Retrieved 20 November 2018 from https://www.reuters.com/article/us-uber-ftc/uber-to-pay-20-million-to-settle-u-s-claims-it-misled-drivers-idUSKBN15334C.

Bauman, Z. 1976. *Socialism: The Active Utopia*. New York: Holmes & Meier Publishers.

Bear, L. 2015. 'Capitalist Divination: Popularist Speculators and Technologies of Imagination on the Hooghly River', *Comparative Studies of South Asia, Africa and the Middle East* 35(3): 408–23.

Bear, L., R. Birla and S.S. Puri. 2015. 'Speculation: Futures and Capitalism in India', *Comparative Studies of South Asia, Africa and the Middle East* 35(3): 387–91.

Bear, L., K. Ho, A. Tsing and S. Yanagisako. 2015. 'Gens: A Feminist Manifesto for the Study of Capitalism'. Retrieved 20 November 2018 from https://culanth.org/fieldsights/652-gens-a-feminist-manifesto-for-the-study-of-capitalism.

Berlant, L. 2011. *Cruel Optimism*. Durham, NC: Duke University Press.

Bernstein, A. 2013. *Religious Bodies Politic: Rituals of Sovereignty in Buryat Buddhism*. Chicago: University of Chicago Press.

Biggart, N.W. 1989. *Charismatic Capitalism: Direct Selling Organizations in America*. Chicago: University of Chicago Press.

Blim, M. 2000. 'Capitalisms in Late Modernity', *Annual Review of Anthropology* 29: 25–38.

Borenstein, E. 1999. 'Public Offerings: MMM and the Marketing of Melodrama', in A.M. Barker (ed.), *Consuming Russia: Popular Culture, Sex, and Society since Gorbachev*. Durham, NC: Duke University Press, pp. 49–75.

Bromley, D.G. 1995. 'Quasi-religious Corporations: A New Integration of Religion and Capitalism?', in R.H. Roberts (ed.), *Religion and the Transformations of Capitalism: Comparative Approaches*. London: Routledge, pp. 135–60.

Brown, D. 2007. 'Marketing Group Merely "Selling a Dream"', *The Times*, 27 November. Retrieved 20 November 2018 from https://www.thetimes.co.uk/article/marketing-group-merely-selling-a-dream-5s6d5jl5zwc.

Burawoy, M. 1979. *Manufacturing Consent: Changes in the Labour Process under Monopoly Capitalism*. Chicago: University of Chicago Press.

———. 1999. 'Afterword', in M. Burawoy and K. Verdery (eds), *Uncertain Transition: Ethnographies of Change in the Postsocialist World*. Lanham, MD: Rowman & Littlefield, pp. 301–12.

Burawoy, M., and K. Verdery (eds). 1999. *Uncertain Transition: Ethnographies of Change in the Postsocialist World*. Lanham, MD: Rowman & Littlefield.

Cahn, P.S. 2006. 'Building down and Dreaming up: Finding Faith in a Mexican Multilevel Marketer', *American Ethnologist* 33(1): 126–42.

———. 2011. *Direct Sales and Direct Faith in Latin America*. New York: Palgrave Macmillan.

Carrier, J.G. 1990. 'The Symbolism of Possession in Commodity Advertising', *Man* 25(4): 693–706.

Clarke, A.J. 1999. *Tupperware: The Promise of Plastic in 1950s America*. Washington, DC: Smithsonian Institution Press.

Coleman, S. 2003. 'Continuous Conversion? The Rhetoric, Practice, and Rhetorical Practice of Charismatic Protestant Conversion', in A. Buckser and S.D. Glazier (eds), *The Anthropology of Religious Conversion*. Oxford: Rowman & Littlefield, pp. 15–28.

Comaroff, J., and J. Comaroff (eds). 2001. *Millennial Capitalism and the Culture of Neoliberalism*. Durham, NC: Duke University Press.

Cross, J., and A. Street. 2009. 'Anthropology at the Bottom of the Pyramid', *Anthropology Today* 25(4): 4–9.
Curtis, G.E. (ed.). 1996. *Russia: A Country Study*. Washington, DC: GPO for the Library of Congress.
De Goede, M. 2005. *Virtue, Fortune and Faith: A Genealogy of Finance*. Minneapolis: University of Minnesota Press.
De Neve, G. 2009. 'Asking for and Giving Baki: Neo-bondage, or the Interpay of Bondage and Resistance in the Tamilnadu Power-Loom Industry', in M. Mollona, G. DeNeve and J. Parry (eds), *Industrial Work and Life: An Anthropological Reader.* Oxford: Berg, pp. 363–83.
De Vidas, A.A. 2008. 'Containing Modernity: The Social Life of Tupperware in a Mexican Indigenous Village', *Ethnography* 9: 257–84.
DeVos, R. 2010. 'Capitalism with Compassion'. Retrieved 20 November 2018 from https://acton.org/pub/religion-liberty/volume-4-number-5/capitalism-compassion.
DeVos, R.M. 1993. *Compassionate Capitalism: People Helping People Help Themselves*. New York: Plume.
Diatlov, V. 2000. *Sovremennye Torgovye Men'shinstva: Faktor Stabil'nosti ili Konflikta?* Moscow: Natalis.
Dolan, C., and M. Johnstone-Louis. 2011. 'Re-siting Corporate Responsibility: The Making of South Africa's Avon Entrepreneurs', *Focaal* 60: 21–33.
Dolan, C., and L. Scott. 2009. 'Lipstick Evangelism: Avon Trading Circles and Gender Empowerment in South Africa', *Gender and Development* 17(2): 203–18.
Douglas, M., and B.C. Isherwood. 2003. *The World of Goods: Towards an Anthropology of Consumption*. London: Routledge.
Dugarzhapova, T. 1987. 'Zhenshchiny Agi – Aktivnye Stroiteli Kommunizma', in T. Sandanov (ed.), *Ekonomicheskoe i Sotsial'noe Razvitie Aginskogo Buriatskogo Avtonomnogo Okruga: Tezisy Dokladov k Predstoiashchei Nauchno-Prakticheskoi Konferentsii, Posviashchennoi 50-letiiu Obrazovaniia Okruga*. Chita.
Dyakina, M. 2013. 'IMF Warns Russia on Increasing Houshold Debt Burden'. Retrieved 3 December 2018 from http://www.reuters.com/article/russia-imf-banking-idUSL5N0IC2GB20131022.
Egorov, E. 2015. 'Komu Pomozhet Zakon o Bankrotstve Fizicheskikh Lits', *Vedomosti*, 13 February. Retrieved 20 November 2018 from http://www.vedomosti.ru/finance/articles/2015/02/13/kak-stat-bankrotom.
Eremina, A., and N. Biianova. 2015. 'Sergei Mavrodi Snova Predlagaet Rossiianam Fantasticheskie Protsenty', *Vedomosti*, 10 February. Retrieved 20 November 2018 from http://www.vedomosti.ru/newspaper/articles/2015/02/10/shestaya-piramida-mavrodi.
Fehérváry, K. 2009. 'Goods and States: The Political Logic of State-Socialist Material Culture', *Comparative Studies in Society and History* 51(2): 426–59.
Ferguson, J. 2015. *Give a Man a Fish: Reflections on the New Politics of Distribution*. Durham, NC: Duke University Press.
Foster, R. 2005. 'Commodity Futures: Labour, Love and Value', *Anthropology Today* 21(4): 8–12.

Foucault, M. 1994. 'Technologies of the Self', in P. Rabinow (ed.), *Ethics: Subjectivity and Truth (Essential Works of Foucault 1954–1984).* London: Penguin, pp. 223–51.

Friedman, W.A. 2004. *Birth of a Salesman: The Transformation of Selling in America.* Cambridge, MA: Harvard University Press.

Fuller, A.C. 1960. *A Foot in the Door.* New York: McGraw-Hill.

Gell, A. 1992. 'Inter-tribal Commodity Barter and Reproductive Gift Exchange in Old Melanesia', in C. Humphrey and S. Hugh-Jones (eds), *Barter, Exchange and Value: An Anthropological Approach.* Cambridge: Cambridge University Press, pp. 142–68.

Gongorov, T. (ed.). 2002. *Nash Obshchii Dom.* Chita: Print-Mysl'.

Granovetter, M. 1985. 'Economic Action and Social Structure', *American Journal of Sociology* 91(3): 481–510.

Gregory, C.A. 1982. *Gifts and Commodities.* London: Academic Press.

Gudeman, S. 2008. *Economy's Tension: Dialectics of Community and Market.* New York: Berghahn Books.

Guseva, A. 2008. *Into the Red: The Birth of the Credit Card Market in Postcommunist Russia.* Stanford: Stanford University Press.

Guyer, J. 2004. *Marginal Gains: Monetary Transactions in Atlantic Africa.* Chicago: University of Chicago Press.

Hann, C. (ed.). 2003. *The Postsocialist Agrarian Question: Property Relations and the Rural Condition.* Münster: LIT.

Hart, K. 2013. 'Making Money with Money: Reflections of a Betting Man', in R. Cassidy, A. Pisac and C. Loussouarn (eds), *Qualitative Research in Gambling: Exploring the Production and Consumption of Risk.* New York: Routledge, pp. 15–27.

Harvey, D. 2005. *A Brief History of Neoliberalism.* Oxford: Oxford University Press.

Herbalife. 2018. 'Herbalife Segodnia'. Retrieved 20 November 2018 from https://herbalife.ru/today.

Ho, K. 2009a. *Liquidated: An Ethnography of Wall Street.* Durham, NC: Duke University Press.

———. 2009b. 'Disciplining Investment Bankers, Disciplining the Economy: Wall Street's Institutional Culture of Crisis and the Downsizing of "Corporate America"', *American Anthropologist* 111(2): 177–89.

Hochschild, A.R. 2012. *The Managed Heart: Commercialization of Human Feeling.* Berkeley: University of California Press.

Højer, L. 2012. 'The Spirit of Business: Pawnshops in Ulaanbaatar', *Social Anthropology* 20(1): 34–49.

Hornby, L. 2015. 'Failed China Schemes Pull down Hundreds of Thousands of Investors', *Financial Times*, 22 September. Retrieved 20 November 2018 from https://next.ft.com/content/cca9d1a2-5da8-11e5-9846-de406ccb37f2.

Humphrey, C. 1998. *Marx Went Away – But Karl Stayed Behind.* Ann Arbor: University of Michigan Press.

———. 1999. 'Traders, "Disorder", and Citizenship in Provincial Russia', in M. Burawoy and K. Verdery (eds), *Uncertain Transition: Ethnographies of Change in the Postsocialist World.* Lanham, MD: Rowman & Littlefield, pp. 19–52.

———. 2000. 'How is Barter Done? The Social Relations of Barter in Provincial Russia', in P. Seabright (ed.), *The Vanishing Rouble: Barter Networks and Non-monetary Transactions in Post-Soviet Societies*. Cambridge: Cambridge University Press, pp. 259–97.

———. 2002. 'Creating a Culture of Disillusionment: Consumption in Moscow, a Chronicle of Changing Times', in *The Unmaking of Soviet Life: Everyday Economies after Socialism*. Ithaca, NY: Cornell University Press, pp. 40–63.

———. 2007. 'New Subjects and Situated Interdependence: After Privatization in Ulan-Ude', in C. Alexander, V. Buchli and C. Humphrey (eds), *Urban Life in Post-Soviet Asia*. London: UCL Press, pp. 175–207.

Humphrey, C., and R. Mandel (eds). 2002. *Markets and Moralities: Ethnographies of Postsocialism*. Oxford: Berg.

Humphrey, C., and D. Sneath. 1999. *The End of Nomadism? Society, State, and the Environment in Inner Asia*. Durham, NC: Duke University Press.

Illouz, E. 2007. *Cold Intimacies: The Making of Emotional Capitalism*. Cambridge: Polity Press.

James, D. 2014. '"Deeper into a Hole?" Borrowing and Lending in South Africa', *Current Anthropology* 55(S9): S17–S29.

Jeffery, L. 2001. 'Selling Selves: Meanings of the Market in the People's Republic of China', Ph.D. dissertation. Santa Cruz: University of California.

Jones, K.A. 2011. *Amway Forever*. Hoboken, NJ: John Wiley & Sons.

Keep, W., and P. Vander Nat. 2014. 'Multilevel Marketing and Pyramid Schemes in the United States', *Journal of Historical Research in Marketing* 6(2): 188–210.

Kelly, M. 2013. 'Foucault, Subjectivity, and Technologies of the Self', in C. Falzon, T. O'Leary and J. Sawicki (eds), *A Companion to Foucault*. Malden, MA: Wiley-Blackwell, pp. 510–25.

Klumbyte, N. 2010. 'The Soviet Sausage Renaissance', *American Anthropologist* 112(1): 22–37.

Kornai, J. 1992. *The Socialist System: The Political Economy of Communism*. Princeton, NJ: Princeton University Press.

Krige, D. 2011. '"We are Running for a Living": Work, Leisure and Speculative Accumulation in an Underground Numbers Lottery in Johannesburg', *African Studies* 70(1): 3–24.

———. 2012. 'Fields of Dreams, Fields of Schemes: Ponzi Finance and Multi-level Marketing in South Africa', *Africa* 82(1): 69–92.

Ledeneva, A.V. 1998. *Russia's Economy of Favours: Blat, Networking, and Informal Exchange*. Cambridge: Cambridge University Press.

———. 2006. *How Russia Really Works: The Informal Practices that Shaped Post-Soviet Politics and Business*. Ithaca, NY: Cornell University Press.

———. 2013. *Can Russia Modernise? Sistema, Power Networks and Informal Governance*. Cambridge: Cambridge University Press.

Lemon, A. 1998. '"Your Eyes are Green Like Dollars": Counterfeit Cash, National Substance, and Currency Apartheid in 1990s Russia', *Cultural Anthropology* 13(1): 22–55.

Lim, L. 2009. 'Pyramid Schemes Proliferate in China', *Npr*, 16 February. Retrieved 29 June 2016 from http://www.npr.org/templates/story/story.php?storyId=99493406.

Lindquist, G. 2006. *Conjuring Hope: Magic and Healing in Contemporary Russia*. New York: Berghahn Books.

Linkhovoin, L. 2012. *Lodon Bagshyn Debterhee: Materialy na Buriatskom i Russkom Iazykakh*. Ulan-Ude: Buriaad-mongol nom.

LiPuma, E., and B. Lee. 2004. *Financial Derivatives and the Globalization of Risk*. Durham, NC: Duke University Press.

Long, J., and K. Graber. 2009. 'The Dissolution of the Buriat Autonomous Okrugs in Siberia', *Inner Asia* 11(1): 147–55.

Loussouarn, C. 2013. 'Spread Betting and the City of London', in R. Cassidy, A. Pisac and C. Loussouarn (eds), *Qualitative Research in Gambling: Exploring the Production and Consumption of Risk*. New York: Routledge, pp. 233–50.

Makhachkeev, A. 2007. *Aginskii Virazh: Kratkii Ekskurs v Noveishuiu Istoriiu Agi*. Ulan-Ude: BNC SO RAN.

Manning, P., and A. Uplisashvili. 2007. '"Our Beer": Ethnographic Brands in Postsocialist Georgia', *American Anthropologist* 109(4): 626–41.

Meillassoux, C. 1981. *Maidens, Meal and Money: Capitalism and the Domestic Community*. Cambridge: Cambridge University Press.

Miller, D. 2001. 'Alienable Gifts and Inalienable Commodities', in F. Myers (ed.), *The Empire of Things: Regimes of Value and Material Culture*. Santa Fe: School of American Research Press, pp. 91–118.

Miyazaki, H. 2003. 'The Temporalities of the Market', *American Anthropologist* 105(2): 255–65.

———. 2013. *Arbitraging Japan: Dreams of Capitalism at the End of Finance*. Berkeley: University of California Press.

Musaraj, S. 2011. 'Tales from Albarado: The Materiality of Pyramid Schemes in Postsocialist Albania', *Cultural Anthropology* 26(1): 84–110.

Nash, J. 1979. *We Eat the Mines and the Mines Eat Us: Dependency and Exploitation in Bolivian Tin Mines*. New York: Columbia University Press.

Neate, R. 2012. 'Herbalife CEO Accused of Running "Ponzi Scheme"', *The Guardian*, 21 December. Retrieved 20 November 2018 from https://www.theguardian.com/world/2012/dec/21/herbalife-ceo-ponzi-scheme.

Nezavisimyi Institut Sotsial'noi Politiki 2004. 'Sotsial'nyi Atlas Rossiiskikh Regionov'. Retrieved 20 November 2018 from http://www.socpol.ru/atlas/portraits/chita.shtml.

Nimaev, D.D. 2004. 'Prisoedinenie Buriatii k Rossii i Nachalo Etnopoliticheskoi Stabilizacii', in L.L. Abaeva and N.L. Zhukovskaia (eds), *Buriaty*. Moscow: Nauka, pp. 38–44.

Nocera, J. 2015. 'The Pyramid Scheme Problem', *New York Times*, 15 September. Retrieved 20 November 2018 from http://www.nytimes.com/2015/09/15/opinion/joe-nocera-the-pyramid-scheme-problem.html?_r=2.

Ong, A. 1987. *Spirits of Resistance and Capitalist Discipline: Factory Women in Malaysia*. Albany: State of New York Press.

Oushakine, S.A. 2014. '"Against the Cult of Things": On Soviet Productivism, Storage Economy, and Commodities with No Destination', *Russian Review* 73: 198–236.

Pedersen, M.A. 2007. 'From "Public" to "Private" Markets in Postsocialist Mongolia', *Anthropology of East Europe Review*, 25(1): 64–71.

Pelkmans, M. 2009. 'Temporary Conversions: Encounters with Pentecostalism in Muslim Kyrgyzstan', in M. Pelkmans (ed.), *Conversion after Socialism: Disruptions, Modernisms, and the Technologies of Faith*. New York: Berghahn Books, pp. 143–61.

Polanyi, K. 1944. *The Great Transformation*. New York: Farrar & Rinehart.

Prokhorov, A.M. (ed.). 1973. *Bol'shaia Sovetskaia Entsiklopediia*. Moscow: Izdatel'stvo Sovetskaia Entsiklopediia.

Puri, S.S. 2015. 'Betting on Performed Futures: Predictive Procedures at Delhi Racecourse', *Comparative Studies of South Asia, Africa and the Middle East* 35(3): 466–80.

Raksina, I. 2013. 'Zhizn' v Kredit', *Novye Izvestiia*, 10 September. Retrieved 20 November 2018 from http://www.newizv.ru/economics/2013-09-19/189238-zhizn-v-kredit.html.

Randalls, S. 2013. 'Weather Trading in London: Distinguishing Finance from Gambling', in R. Cassidy, A. Pisac and C. Loussouarn (eds), *Qualitative Research in Gambling: Exploring the Production and Consumption of Risk*. New York: Routledge, pp. 187–201.

Robbins, J. 2004. 'The Globalization of Pentecostal and Charismatic Christianity', *Annual Review of Anthropology* 33: 117–43.

Rona-Tas, A., and A. Guseva. 2014. *Plastic Money: Constructing Markets for Credit Cards in Eight Postcommunist Countries*. Stanford: Stanford University Press.

Rudenko, P., and O. Volkova 2013. 'Dolgovaia Karta Rossii: Gde Zhivut Samye Zakreditovannye Rossiiane', *Forbes*, 11 September. Retrieved 20 November 2018 from http://www.forbes.ru/infographics/finansy/igroki/244502-dolgovaya-karta-rossii-gde-zhivut-samye-zakreditovannye-rossiyane.

Rudnyckyj, D. 2009. 'Spiritual Economies: Islam and Neoliberalism in Contemporary Indonesia', *Cultural Anthropology* 24(1): 104–41.

Sahlins, M. 1972. *Stone Age Economics*. New York: Aldine Publishing Company.

Samuel, L. 2012. *The American Dream: A Cultural History*. Syracuse, NY: Syracuse University Press.

Sandanov, T. 2004. *Formirovanie Mestnogo Samoupravleniia v Aginskom Buriatskom Avtonomnom Okruge, Ego Rol' v Zhizni Naseleniia (1990–2004 gg.)*. Ulan-Ude: GOU VSTAKI.

Savel'ev, K. 2013. 'V Kaluge Raskryli Novuiu Finansovuiu Piramidu', *Vesti*, 21 February. Retrieved 20 November 2018 from http://www.vesti.ru/doc.html?id=1037658.

Shagdarov, B., and Z. Dorzhiev. 1971. Aga Stepnaia: Razvitie Khoziaistva i Kul'tury Aginskogo Buriatskogo Natsional'nogo Okruga za Gody Sovetskoi Vlasti. Ulan-Ude: Buriatskoe knizhnoe izdatel'stvo.

Smirnova, J. 2012. 'Dreistes Comback des Finanzpyramiden-Moguls', *Die Welt*, 25 April. Retrieved 20 November 2018 from http://www.welt.de/vermischtes/article106222605/Dreistes-Comeback-des-Finanzpyramiden-Moguls.html.

Sneath, D. 2006. 'Transacting and Enacting: Corruption, Obligation and the Use of Monies in Mongolia', *Ethnos* 71(1): 89–112.

———. 2012. 'The "Age of the Market" and the Regime of Debt: The Role of Credit in the Transformation of Pastoral Mongolia', *Social Anthropology* 20(4): 458–73.

Stanley, A. 1996. 'Avon and Mary Kay Create Opportunities for Women', *New York Times*, 14 August. Retrieved 20 November 2018 from http://www.nytimes.com/1996/08/14/business/avon-and-mary-kay-create-opportunities-for-women.html?pagewanted=all.

Tataurov, G. 2006. *Vzgliad iz Proshlogo*. Aginskoe: Izdatel'skii dom Agyn Unen.

Taussig, M. 1980. *The Devil and Commodity Fetishism in South America*. Chapel Hill: University of North Carolina Press.

Tereshina, D. 2013. 'Topos "Amerikanskoi Mechty": Seminary, Seti i Setevoi Marketing Kompanii "Amway"', in N. Ssorin-Chaikov (ed.), *Topografiia Schast'ia*. Moscow: Novoe literaturnoe obozrenie, pp. 130–70.

Toboev, T. 2011. 'Proshlaia Istoriia Khorinskikh i Aginskikh Buriat', in C.P. Vanchikova, S. Chimitdorzhiev and M.V. Aiusheeva (eds), *Buriatskie Letopisi*. Ulan-Ude: OAO Respublikanskaia tipografiia, pp. 8–31.

Tsing, A. 2005. *Friction: An Ethnography of Global Connection*. Princeton, NJ: Princeton University Press.

Tsydenova, D. 2009. *Predstavleniia Aginskikh Buriat o Zhizni i Smerti (Konets XIX-Nachalo XXI V.)*. Novosibirsk: Redaktsionno-izdatel'skii tsentr NGU.

Tumunov, Z. 2006. *Istoriia Agi 1648–1917*. Ulan-Ude: Respublikanskaia tipografiia.

Tupperware, 2018. 'O Kompanii'. Retrieved 20 November 2018 from http://www.tupperware.ru/o-nas/o-kompanii.

Valentine, D. 1998. 'Pyramid Schemes'. Retrieved 20 November from https://www.ftc.gov/public-statements/1998/05/pyramid-schemes.

Vasil'eva, A.S. 2011. 'Osobennosti Potrebitel'skogo Kreditovaniia v Rossii v Sovremennykh Usloviiakh', *Bankovskoe Delo* 38: 27–38.

Verdery, K. 1996. *What was Socialism, and What Comes Next?* Princeton, NJ: Princeton University Press.

———. 2003. *The Vanishing Hectare: Property and Value in Postsocialist Transylvania*. Ithaca, NY: Cornell University Press.

Wanner, C. 2009. 'Conversion and the Mobile Self: Evangelicalism as "Travelling Culture"', in M. Pelkmans (ed.), *Conversion after Socialism: Disruptions, Modernisms, and the Technologies of Faith*. New York: Berghahn Books, pp. 163–82.

Watson, J.L. (ed.). 2006. *Golden Arches East: McDonald's in East Asia*. Stanford: Stanford University Press.

Weber, M. 2002. *The Protestant Ethic and the Spirit of Capitalism*. Oxford: Blackwell.

Weiner, A.B. 1992. *Inalienable Possessions: The Paradox of Keeping-While-Giving*. Berkeley: University of California Press.

White, J.B. 1994. *Money Makes Us Relatives: Women's Labor in Urban Turkey*. Austin: University of Texas Press.

Wilson, A. 1999. 'The Empire of Direct Sales and the Making of Thai Entrepreneurs', *Critique of Anthropology* 19: 401–22.

———. 2004. *The Intimate Economies of Bangkok: Tomboys, Tycoons, and Avon Ladies in the Global City*. Berkeley: University of California Press.

Woodruff, D. 1999. 'The Barter of the Bankrupt', in M. Burawoy and K. Verdery (eds), *Uncertain Transition: Ethnographies of Change in the Postsocialist World*. Lanham, MD: Rowman & Littlefield, pp. 83–124.

World Federation of Direct Selling Associations (2018a). 'Global Direct Selling: 2017 Retail Sales'. Retrieved 17 August 2018 from www.wfdsa.org.

———. (2018b). 'Global Sales by Product Category: 2017'. Retrieved 17 August 2018 from www.wfdsa.org.

Yanagisako, S.J. 2002. *Producing Culture and Capital: Family Firms in Italy*. Princeton, NJ: Princeton University Press.

Yang, M.M. 1994. *Gifts, Favors, and Banquets: The Art of Social Relationships in China*. Ithaca, NY: Cornell University Press.

———. 2000. 'Putting Global Capitalism in its Place: Economic Hybridity, Bataille, and Ritual Expenditure', *Current Anthropology* 41(4): 477–509.

Yurchak, A. 2003. 'Russian Neoliberal: The Entrepreneurial Ethic and the Spirit of "True Careerism"', *Russian Review* 62(1): 72–90.

———. 2006. *Everything was Forever until it was No More: The Last Soviet Generation*. Princeton, NJ: Princeton University Press.

Zabaikalkraistat (Rosstat). 2013. 'Aginskii Buriatskii Okrug v Tsifrakh'. Statisticheskii Sbornik (statistical yearbook).

Zaloom, C. 2006. *Out of the Pits: Traders and Technology from Chicago to London*. Chicago: University of Chicago Press.

———. 2009. 'How to Read the Future? The Yield Curve, Affect, and Financial Prediction', *Public Culture* 21(2): 245–68.

Zamakhina, T. 2015. 'Za Sozdanie Finansovoi Piramidy Oshtrafuiut na Million', *Rossiskaia Gazeta*, 2 December. Retrieved 20 November 2018 from https://rg.ru/2015/12/02/piramida-site-anons.html.

Zelizer, V. 2005. *The Purchase of Intimacy*. Princeton, NJ: Princeton University Press.

Index

www.ingramcontent.com/pod-product-compliance
Ingram Content Group UK Ltd.
Pitfield, Milton Keynes, MK11 3LW, UK
UKHW021344130926
8556IPUK00047B/438

9 781789 200126